I0128449

Honoring Ancestors in Sacred Space

Florida Museum of Natural History: Ripley P. Bullen Series

FLORIDA MUSEUM.

HONORING ANCESTORS IN
Sacred Space

The Archaeology of an Eighteenth-Century
African-Bahamian Cemetery

GRACE TURNER

University of Florida Press
Gainesville

Copyright 2017 by Grace Turner
All rights reserved
Published in the United States of America

First cloth printing, 2017
First paperback printing, 2023

28 27 26 25 24 23   6 5 4 3 2 1

Library of Congress Cataloging-in-Publication Data
Names: Turner, Grace, author.
Title: Honoring ancestors in sacred space : the archaeology of an
eighteenth-century African-Bahamian cemetery / Grace Turner.
Other titles: Ripley P. Bullen series.
Description: Gainesville : University of Florida Press, 2017. | Series:
Florida Museum of Natural History: Ripley P. Bullen series | Includes
bibliographical references and index.
Identifiers: LCCN 2017010460 | ISBN 9781683400202 (cloth) | ISBN 9781683404040 (pbk.)
Subjects: LCSH: Blacks—Bahamas—Nassau—Antiquities. |
Cemeteries—Bahamas—Nassau. | Ethnoarchaeology—Bahamas—Nassau. |
Excavations (Archaeology)—Bahamas—Nassau. | African diaspora. | Nassau
(Bahamas)—Antiquities.
Classification: LCC F1659.N3 T87 2017 | DDC 972.96—dc23
LC record available at https://lccn.loc.gov/2017010460

University of Florida Press
2046 NE Waldo Road
Suite 2100
Gainesville, FL 32609
http://upress.ufl.edu

UF PRESS

UNIVERSITY
OF FLORIDA

To the memory of my parents,
Chilean and Edna Turner (née Pinder).
They had to forego many of their personal dreams
but always encouraged their children
to dream their own dreams and pursue them.

CONTENTS

FIGURES

TABLES

Introduction

Basic Assumptions

In his seminal work *The Souls of Black Folk*, W. E. B. Du Bois referred to the worlds "within and without the veil" to convey the ambivalent space people of African descent had to live in. He called it a "double consciousness." African-descended people throughout the Americas have historically dealt with this issue. For Bahamians of African descent, the reality of Dubois's concept of double consciousness may no longer have been very clear in their daily lives by the late twentieth and early twenty-first centuries. But for myself, as an archaeologist from a non–North American or Western European cultural background, the distinctions between these "worlds" and world views remain vividly apparent.

"Double consciousness," I feel, more closely portrays the cultural interchange that was displayed in the Northern Burial Ground for over a century and changed as the communities who used it saw the need to adjust or revise their world view. The significance of this is that for much of the twentieth century, anthropologists engaged in a debate about the process of cultural change for African-descended people in the Americas. The catalyst for this debate was the publication of sociologist E. Franklin Frazier's first major work, *The Negro Family in the United States*, in 1939. Frazier, who was African American, argued that the harsh experience of slavery left African Americans devoid of any African cultural heritage. In 1941, in *The Myth of the Negro Past*, anthropologist Melville J. Herskovits made the case that despite the trauma of racialized enslavement, African-descended people in the Americas continued to retain cultural influences from Africa. Sidney Mintz revived the debate with the 1974 publication of his work *Caribbean*

Transformations, in which he made the case for creolization. This understanding of the process of cultural continuation and change gives more weight to the role of innovation and change. Mintz noted that Africans who were brought to the Americas "could and did create viable patterns of life, for which their pasts were pools of available symbolic and material resources" ([1974] 2006, 12). This was an acknowledgement of Herskovits's argument for African retentions, or "Africanisms." However, for Mintz, cultural continuity and change for African-descended people in the Americas involved the reshaping of African-derived cultural resources to create new cultural configurations. As Mintz explained, "Folklore, dance forms, cuisine, music, aesthetic traditions, language, and all else that is cultural require no genetic transmission—only a readiness to learn new forms. These forms, moreover, may be taken on with their old meanings or with new meanings added; in fragments (a word, an exclamation, a gesture) or in 'complexes'; to replace or supplement older forms or, perhaps most commonly, to intermix in some way with them" (Mintz [1974] 2006, 11).

As anthropology developed as a discipline, anthropologists came to understand that while human cultures experience some level of continuity, change also occurs continuously. The challenge for anthropologists is to recognize this process and identify how change unfolded for African-descended people in the Americas. As Mintz stated, "Enslaved Africans carried their cultural heritages into the inferno of slavery with a very different commitment to their ancestral societies than that of the unenslaved. These heritages, in fact, could be maintained in the new settings only by innovativeness and flexibility" ([1974] 2006, 15–16).

By the late twentieth century and into the early twenty-first century, North American anthropologists of African descent were adding their voices to these discussions. These scholars applaud research on African diaspora sites that incorporates the perspective of African-descended people from documentary records but also engages descendant communities for insight into the cultural use and meaning of objects, locations, and landscapes. Such culturally informed insight facilitates more thorough understandings and interpretations of past cultural behavior (Singleton and Bograd 1995, 29; Perry and Paynter 1999, 303; Battle-Baptiste 2011; Fennell 2014; Ogundiran and Saunders 2014, 14).

While I acknowledge such theoretical developments in anthropology, I felt that as a person of African descent, it was important for me to not simply repeat the usual mantra of creolization. The greater significance for me, as the first Bahamian historical archaeologist, was to approach this issue by examining the materiality of a creolizing process as it unfolded through the eyes of an archaeologist. Du Bois's concept of double consciousness most aptly conveyed the challenge people of African descent faced in regard to how to position themselves within the larger social order.

While there was considerable positive social, economic, and political change for African-descended people in the Americas during the second half of the twentieth century, subtle reminders remain of the need to move between worlds of differing cultural meaning. I characterize these worlds in the Bahamas as being of "standard English" and "Bahamian dialect." It is true that these divisions are heavily impacted by social class, economic status, and education, but for people of the African Diaspora, these factors have historically been colored by issues of socially ascribed race.

Although this is a work within the academic discipline of anthropology, I also wanted to ensure that it was also pertinent to a Bahamian audience of mostly non-anthropologists. To date there are only a handful of anthropology publications on the Bahamas. These include the cultural work Rosalyn Howard did with the descendants of Black Seminoles (2002) and work in historical archaeology by Laurie Wilkie and Paul Farnsworth (2005). For this publication, I not only wanted to explore questions and issues pertinent to archaeology of the African Diaspora, I also wanted to be supportive of my audience of fellow Bahamians. For this audience, I opted to retain some details such as the section that explains the Lucayan component of the research site.

This work examines an African-Bahamian urban cemetery that was used from the early eighteenth century to the early twentieth century. I look at how these communities shaped and changed this cemetery landscape to reflect the complexities of their lives over time. Because the material expressions of the cemetery landscape represent the cultural perspectives of the affiliated communities, so changes in its maintenance can be seen as archaeological evidence of this process (Perry and Paynter 1999; McCarthy 2006; Blouet 2014; Fennell 2014; Matternes and Richey 2014; Ogundiran and Saunders 2014).

My intention was to identify and demonstrate evidence of significant variations in experiences within the African Diaspora. Although the majority of Africans and their descendants in the Americas lived on plantations, that was not the only life experience in this Diaspora. Black urban laborers, enslaved or free, often had greater opportunity to organize their personal lives to suit their purposes than those who were restricted by the demands an owner or overseer imposed. Although I attribute some action to the individual agency of eighteenth-century African-Bahamians in Nassau, the British colonial government had a different perspective than white urban elites and planters about how to deal with African-descended people. The role of the colonial government in mediating the status of non-whites had a significant impact on how free people of color and enslaved urban laborers were able to conduct their lives.

For archaeologists, a second issue is being able to identify the African-influenced landscapes these involuntary immigrants created. Even though Africans were accorded the lowest social status, that did not preclude them from expressing their perspectives of the world in which they lived. Archaeological assessments of culturally meaningful landscapes help demonstrate the extent to which Africans in the Atlantic Diaspora were able to impress their world view on the landscape. Within the general context of a European-style cemetery site, people of African descent were able to express African-influenced concepts of memorializing the dead. Any perceived change in this cultural behavior can be interpreted as a reflection of changes in the world view of these African-Bahamians.

Most historical archaeology research in the Caribbean has aimed at understanding the nature of enslavement in the context of plantations. Yet the plantation experience was only one aspect of the Atlantic Diaspora. Archaeological research in non-plantation contexts can expand our knowledge of the lived experiences of African-descended people throughout the Americas.

Mortuary aspects of a cemetery landscape can be used to examine the physical impact of distinctive urban African-Bahamian lives, but the sample excavated from this site is so small it would not be representative of the community that used the cemetery. Instead, the emphasis is on the cultural meaning of material remains and the environmental treatment of the space. I make the case that Africans in the Atlantic Diaspora were able, to varying extents, to create a world for themselves "within the veil" that was not modeled on European cultural systems to which they had been transposed. This world within the veil was modeled on an understanding of life drawn from their African cultural heritage. The behavior of a subcultural group is visibly lived out within the larger society, but for those who are unaware of the meanings and significance of these cultural signs and symbols, this sub-cultural behavior is invisible, or at least is not understood and is therefore ignored. From this perspective, the world "without the veil" represented their place within the wider, dominant society, where, until 1834 in British colonies in the Atlantic and the Caribbean, people of African descent were either enslaved or free. This perspective recognizes that Africans in the Diaspora continuously made cultural decisions, depending on their life circumstances, about the extent to which they moved between these different worlds or even if they chose to move at all (Perry and Paynter 1999; McCarthy 2006; Young 2007; Fennell 2014; Gómez 2014; Norman 2014; Reeves 2014).

The concept of double consciousness involves a cultural awareness of two distinct worlds and world views. One of these states of consciousness reflects a European cultural heritage; the other involves the interaction of African-descended people with the many forms of European society and cultural heritage. It is at such intersections that one sees the myriad nego-tiations between different forms of cultural heritage. It should be expected that despite their low status in the wider society, Africans in the Diaspora made cultural decisions about the form and extent of their cultural inter-actions over time. Some material evidence of these interactions remains visible in the archaeological record.

Although their movement was involuntary, Africans were, nevertheless, a migrant group to the Americas. Their responses and adjustments to life in a new environment were modeled on behavior drawn from their cultures of origin. Enslaved individuals were severely restricted in the extent to which they were free to manage many aspects of their daily lives. However, ar-chaeological research on African-descended populations illustrates some of the ways that enslaved and free Africans and their descendants crafted distinct identities for themselves (Armstrong and Fleischman 2003; Fergu-son 1992; Heath and Bennett 2000; Samford 2000; McCarthy 2006; Blouet 2014; Matternes and Richey 2014). Archaeological research on enslaved and free Africans in urban contexts has the potential to provide greater insight about the ways Africans in the Diaspora were able to create lifeways that relied heavily on their African cultural heritage.

Less archaeological research has focused on Africans in urban environ-ments, where it is more difficult to identify groups definitively by race or ethnicity than it is for groups on plantations (Rankin-Hill 1997; David-son 2004; Farmer, Smith, and Watson 2005; Blakey and Rankin-Hill 2009; Perry, Howson, and Bianca 2009; Medford 2009). This was especially so in the case of enslaved workers who were limited in their ability to leave a distinctive footprint on their living and/or work spaces.

Most African Diaspora archaeology in urban contexts has been done on cemetery sites (Davidson 2004; Perry, Howson, and Bianca 2009; McCar-thy 1997; Farmer, Smith, and Watson 2005). Cemetery sites are representa-tive of the entire community they served and therefore can provide details about the physical, social, economic, and cultural lives of the people within that community. This examination of a Bahamian urban mortuary context allows for possible comparisons with other African Diaspora sites of urban archaeology.

Research Background

The Northern Burial Ground for Blacks and Persons of Colour[1] was situ-ated on the waterfront that faces Hog Island (now Paradise Island) on the eastern edge of the town of Nassau. It was one of five public cemeteries con-secrated in May 1826. Three of these cemeteries were located on the eastern side of the town and the other two were immediately west of Nassau. The petition for consecration stated that all of these cemeteries had been in use for over twenty years.

Each of these cemeteries served a specific purpose. The Anglican Church established St. Matthew's Parish on the eastern side of Nassau in 1792 to accommodate the increase in population after Loyalists migrated to the Bahamas in the 1780s. The churchyard served as a cemetery. In addition, Centre Burial Ground was established in the early 1700s; today it is the earliest known cemetery in Nassau. The Northern Burial Ground is located across East Bay Street from Centre Burial Ground. It was originally sited at the water's edge, but in the early 1960s this shoreline was filled in to cre-ate about 100 feet of land between the earlier water's edge and the current shoreline.

Knowledge of the Northern Burial Ground site and awareness of its sig-nificance in Bahamian history and culture were stymied by two factors that caused it to remain obscured even though it is situated in a very public location. It was physically obscured through much of the twentieth century after it was covered over by the storm surge from hurricanes in the late 1920s. Additionally, documentary evidence on the cemetery during its history from the late eighteenth to early nineteenth centuries was not located in the Bahamas but in Jamaica's national archives. This arrangement reflected the organizational hierarchy of the Anglican Church in these two former British West Indian colonies. From 1824, when the Diocese of Jamaica was formally created, until 1861 when the Bahamas became a separate diocese, the administration of the Anglican Church in the Bahamas was headquartered in Jamaica. Because public cemeteries in the Bahamas were managed by the Anglican Church, many of even the most mundane records are now found in the Jamaica Archives.

Since the 1990s several attempts have been made through the Bahamas Department of Archives in Nassau to have signage posted at the cemetery that provides a history of this site. However, any number of logistical hurdles hampered this objective. In the Bahamas, especially for the city of Nassau, there was a growing recognition by the late twentieth century of the economic and cultural value of historic preservation, but preservation needs must also be balanced with the ongoing need for modern development. To earn recognition for preservation, it is necessary to establish the cultural and historical significance of a site, and this can be especially challenging for seemingly vacant land such as this cemetery site (Table 0.1).

A government agency planned to put in an access point across the grass verge for a truck weigh station on the reclaimed land. This weigh station was to check heavy-duty truck traffic before getting onto the Sir Sidney Poitier Bridge, which is located immediately east of the site and allows vehicles to access Paradise Island. Because there was no physical evidence of the cemetery above ground, it was difficult to justify preserving the site only on the basis of documentary evidence, and given the site's history in the first half of the twentieth century the primary challenge in making the case for its preservation was to provide physical evidence of its history as a cemetery. Residents of the nearby community are still aware that there was once a cemetery in this vicinity but they are not clear about its exact location. For those in the community who still knew of this old cemetery's existence, the general understanding was that it was located on land that is currently at the water's edge. However, this area was filled in and reclaimed in the early 1960s.

On New Providence, there is an ugly history of destroying historic cem-

Table 0.1. Timeline for the Northern Burial Ground site

Ca. 1730s	Cemetery is likely established by an urban black community on the eastern side of Nassau
Ca. 1790s	The Northern Burial Ground is incorporated as part of the public cemeteries managed and administered from the new Anglican parish of St. Matthew's
May 1826	Rt. Rev. Christopher Lipscombe, bishop of Jamaica, formally consecrates the cemetery as St. Matthew's Northern Burial Ground for Blacks and People of Colour
June 1833	Gov. B. T. Balfour instructed Anglican clergy to stop using racialized terms in reference to cemeteries
Ca. 1840s	The African-derived cultural practice of placing personal items on top of graves is discontinued
Ca. 1905	St. Matthew's Northern Burial Ground is closed for use as a burial ground
1926, 1929	The Northern Burial Ground is inundated by storm surges from the hurricanes that devastated New Providence in these years. In 1929, the local government was so overwhelmed by the extent of the cleanup that old unused cemeteries such as Centre Burial Ground and the Northern Burial Ground were not restored.
Ca. 1930s	A public sidewalk is constructed through the length of the Northern Burial Ground Site. In preparation for this construction, the shallow burials and associated grave goods are gathered and deposited off site. There is no public outcry to protest the desecration of this old cemetery.
Ca. 1960	About 100 feet of land is filled in beyond the 1880s sea wall that protected the Northern Burial Ground from storm surges
Ca. 2007	A government agency has plans to construct a truck weigh station on the reclaimed land with access from the street through what remained of the Northern Burial Ground Site
August 2007	A ground-penetrating radar survey is conducted over the area of reclaimed land and the grass verge that was originally the Northern Burial Ground
July 2008	A test unit is excavated in the hope of providing archaeological evidence that evidence of the historic cemetery still remained
July and August 2009	Further excavations are conducted to get a better understanding of the history of the site

eteries. In the early twentieth century, Christ Church's cemetery in downtown Nassau, which had been in use since the late seventeenth century, was destroyed to build a commercial structure. Although the headstones were saved and stored in the gardens of Christ Church Cathedral, there was apparently no public outcry in response to this desecration. This may have been because so many of the descendants of this earlier population were either dead or had emigrated elsewhere. In contrast, in 1991, when a black cemetery (Marshallview Cemetery) was bulldozed, the public outrage was so extensive that no one wanted to take responsibility for authorizing the destruction. Marshallview Cemetery was opened in 1892 and had served Nassau's expanding suburban population for nearly 100 years.

One objective of this research was to generate more public awareness of this historic cemetery site and its significance. With current knowledge of the cemetery's location so limited, a ground-penetrating radar (GPR) survey was conducted over the area of reclaimed land and the grass verge to help identify its likely area. (Aerial photographs of this area, the first dating to the 1940s, were discovered after the GPR survey had been done.) A test unit was laid out on the surface above a deeply buried anomaly that was noted in this survey; this test unit was done to allow a preview of the archaeological context of the site. With so little documentation on the history of the Northern Burial Ground, archaeological research would be the primary means of learning more about its history and its social and cultural significance.

The next phase entailed excavating units randomly located across the length of the site to see how the archaeological context was similar or different in different areas of the site. The crew who assisted with the test unit were three Haitian workmen who were experienced in all manner of handiwork except archaeological excavation. Nevertheless, they understood the seriousness of their role in helping reclaim historical recognition for these long-dead individuals. For the more extensive excavations across the site, the field crew consisted of two teams of energetic teenagers in high school and college. They too recognized the part they played in helping respectfully uncover this long-lost aspect of Bahamian history.

Sand that was excavated was screened using quarter-inch mesh screens. Given the inexperience of my field crews and the limited time I had for lab processing, it was necessary to review most finds in the field. This project was an archaeological salvage operation. The original cemetery context had been severely compromised, so I decided to not collect certain categories of artifacts and ecofacts. These included brick fragments because these were no longer in context and were bulky and presented a storage challenge in the limited space in the lab. I also originally planned to eliminate animal bones; in the archaeological literature there was no reference for animal bones as evidence of food that might have been left for the spirit of deceased ancestors to consume. However, it was fortunate that the inexperienced crew brought to my attention some butchered animal bones that did not seem to fit in the same category as twentieth-century machine-cut pork chop bones or whole bones from a chicken wing. As this site has been a public pedestrian walkway for much of the twentieth century, I expected that any animal bones would be evidence of this later period when the cemetery was no longer in use.

Since this was also a waterlogged site because it was originally at the water's edge, all excavated materials were desalinated in fresh water and then air-dried. Interpretation of this site entailed comparisons of physical features that are still visible at a contemporary cemetery site on the west side of Nassau. Other comparisons were made with nineteenth- and twentieth-century cemeteries on other Bahamian islands and with other African Diaspora cemeteries.

1

An Overview of Bahamian History in Context

The first British settlers came to the Bahamas in 1648. This colony, established by the Company of Eleutherian Adventurers like other English colonies, was intended to earn profits for investors and provide a living for participants. It is uncertain whether any of the seventy original settlers were people of African heritage. The colony was never as successful as its organizers had hoped. By the 1650s, some settlers had returned to Bermuda or relocated to other British colonies. Bermudian colonists evidently regarded the small Bahamian colony as a convenient location for banishing their social rejects. These included several whites, such as an unfaithful wife and a Quaker woman who wanted to preach (Lefroy 1981, 133, 227–228; Craton and Saunders 1992, 78). A number of free blacks and enslaved persons were also sent to the Bahamas. In 1656, after the disclosure of a plot by slaves and free blacks to free themselves from white domination, all free blacks in Bermuda were banished to Eleuthera (Wilkinson 1958, 280; Packwood 1975, 142; Lefroy 1981, 94–96; Maxwell 1999, 5).

Documentary evidence of the lives of early Bahamian settlers is rare. It is uncertain how many white inhabitants came to the Bahamas as indentured servants or as tenants to wealthy investor-landlords. This was not a prosperous colony, so it is unlikely that there ever were significant numbers of indentured servants in the Bahamas. As was usual with colonial settlements, there was much speculative optimism about the colony's potential (Sainsbury [1889] 1964, 9, 971; Oldmixon [1741] 1969, 430–431).

Yet even this small struggling colony warranted the importation of unfree African labor. With the evolution of a colonial society also came the changing positions of social groups. The deportation of an entire community of free blacks brought as much change to Bermuda as it did to the

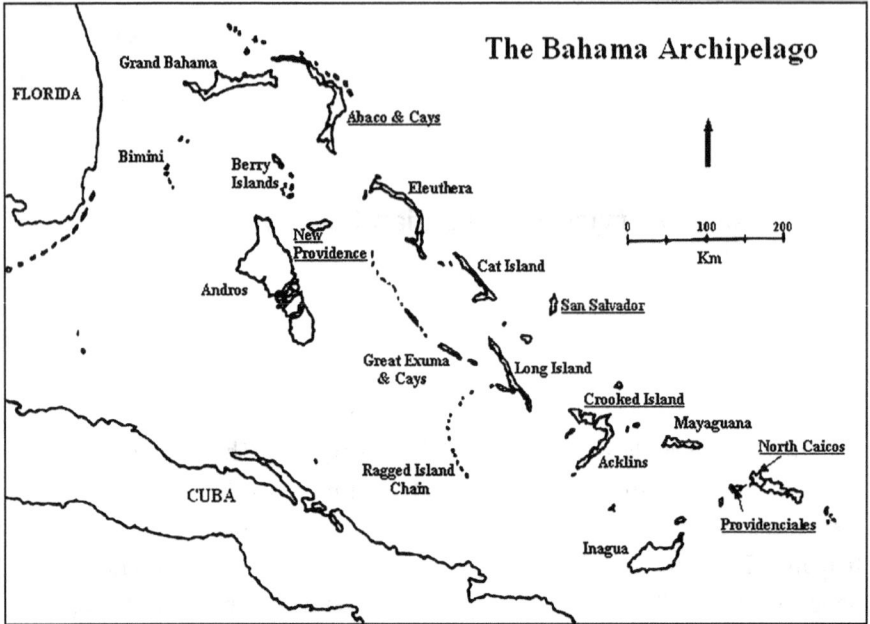

Figure 1.1. The Bahama Archipelago.

Bahamas. In the Bahamas, the many small islands had already proven more suitable to small-scale, independent holdings than the large-scale ventures colonial investors expected would bring them huge profits. This type of setting allowed for an atmosphere that was less restrictive for lower-ranked social groups such as people of color. In this chapter, I examine the basis of economic wealth in the Bahamas and determine whether any avenues existed for African-Bahamians to access this wealth. This review looks at the conditions of life for Bahamians of African heritage in combination with other factors that affected their life conditions over time.

In her book *Race in North America: Origin and Evolution of a Worldview*, biological anthropologist, Audrey Smedley (1999) argued that the cultural history of English settlers in North America contributed to the rigid racial categorization of enslavement for people of African descent and that in contrast, in Spanish and Portuguese South American colonies, racial categorization was more fluid, depending on economic and social circumstances. However, this argument is most true for the British colonies that became the United States. The character of the race-based slave labor system in British

West Indian colonies such as the Bahamas was more similar to the flexible racial characterization of Latin American colonies (Eastwood 2006, 68–73; Helg 2004, 162–167; LaCerte 1993, 42; Lasso 2007, 16–67; Levine 1997, 7–25; Marshall 1993, 16; Beckles 2011, 212; Scarano 2011, 179–183; Wade 1993, 3–14). I make the case that since English colonists also settled the Bahamas, the difference in racial characterization was affected by the paths to wealth and power that were available to all social groups in the Bahamas.

While access to economic and social opportunity may have been restricted for people of color, there was no definitive prohibition against people of African descent participating at different social and economic levels. Nevertheless, access to the most powerful roles and property were heavily protected by social conventions that determined suitable social relationships. These social mores also impacted access to economic opportunities. In the eighteenth century, several acts "for governing Negroes, Mulattoes or Indians" sought to define which persons were categorized in each group. These laws were also reactions to such customary practices as extensive racial and social mixing and the habit of enslaved individuals of working unclaimed land for themselves (Craton and Saunders 1992, 148–156). As blacks constituted at least half the population of the Bahamas from the early eighteenth century forward, it was more feasible for people of color to participate in all but the most power-laden aspects of social, economic, and political life.

For at least the next century after the Bermuda blacks were deported to the Bahamas, people of African descent played significant roles in most levels of Bahamian life. In 1696, an incident occurred that cost proprietary governor Nicholas Trott his career. He was charged with accepting fees and "gifts" to allow Henry Every, alias Bridgeman, to land in Nassau. Every was considered a notorious pirate because he had plundered a ship belonging to the Great Mogul of India (Defoe 1999, 53; Oldmixon [1741] 1969, 429). The decision to land in Nassau was not a random one, as at least four of the white crewmen were "married and are settled upon the Island; and also there came severall boys and foure free negros."[1] This case demonstrates that both white and black Bahamians were tied into at least one global network of profit, albeit not one of the most desirable ones.

The royal charter for the earliest English settlers in the Bahamas detailed an economy based on collecting economically valuable resources from the land and the sea. Because the Bahamas were located along several major sailing routes, the list of legitimate maritime activities included salvaging wrecked and stranded vessels. Until the early eighteenth century, Spanish authorities in Cuba considered much of this activity to be piracy. In the late eighteenth century, newspaper notices indicated that some wrecking activity was done illegally.[2]

There is very little documentary information until the mid-eighteenth century on the general populace and their daily lives. In the leadup to the war in the American colonies, the British had considerable interest in assessing the demographic, economic, and military state of the Bahama Islands. The general conclusion was that they did not have very much soil, that these soils were not very fertile, and that agriculture was not a priority for white settlers. The predominantly transitory nature of the Bahamian economy had fostered a strong sense of independence among settlers (Craton and Saunders 1992, 75–79; Sainsbury [1889] 1964, 7, 712).

Although the Bahamas remained a small and poor colony, because the archipelago was strategically located on major oceanic shipping routes, it was in the interest of the British colonial government to maintain control of these islands. In the eighteenth century, competition for access and control of territory in the Americas was vital for European states that wanted to engage in the struggle for political and economic dominance. The great value of the Bahamas to the British was that its location enabled them to maintain access to the Florida Straits, a major shipping channel for returning to Europe that also connected routes to other parts of the Americas. Gov. Montfort Browne summarized it well in a 1775 report: "They [the Bahamas] command the Gulph of Florida, through which all Spanish vessels with their Treasure return to Europe, As too do the Windward passage; where all ships bound to the West Indies must pass. Their Consequence in this respect has been clearly manifested by the astonishing number of Captures made in those Seas by our privateers War, and the galling Effect it has had on the trade of our Enemys."[3]

By the latter half of the eighteenth century, a critical issue for the Bahamas' colonial government was how to enable settlers (these would generally be white settlers) to obtain title for private land. In a 1768 report to the Earl of Hillsborough, the secretary of state for the colonies, Gov. Thomas Shirley, noted that "Some of the Inhabitants of New Providence especially in the Town of Nassau hold their Land by Grants from the Lords Proprietors and the Company or Copartners for settling the Bahama Islands, and the rest by Grants from the different Governors, that have been in these Islands since their being erected into a Royal Government; but the Inhabitants of the other Islands have no other title to the Lands they hold other than possession."[4] The governor's report was to be sent on to the Board of Trade. Gov. Shirley wanted to stress the urgent need to upgrade the legal basis for private property ownership in the colony. In a letter to the Earl of Hillsborough, the governor explained that "It is needless for me to observe to your Lordship the necessity there is that Government should immediately take some Steps towards securing to the Inhabitants their Property; as I find from their Alarms upon that head, and from the very languid State of the Trade of these Islands, upon which their very Existence depends, many Families have, and still continue to remove from hence to the Continent, and Neighbouring Islands."[5] In 1670, administration of the Bahama Islands was transferred from the Company of Eleutherian Adventurers to the six lord proprietors of the Carolinas. However, in the transition from a proprietary colony to a Crown colony in 1718, the Crown did not include a buyout of the lord proprietors' title to lands of the colony. About fifty years later, Gov. Browne's exasperation was evident in his assessment of the consequences of this situation:

> There are many cogent reasons, my Lord, why the Bahama Islands can never arrive to any state of real advantage to the Crown, until the property of the Islands can be secured to the Planter; For until that happy period arrives, no Inhabitant, wood cutter, or planter can ever be confined to his own plantation. These people now range from Island to Island, and so soon as the Land in one place refuses to yield its increase agreeable to their Expectations, Or the Timber by its distance from the place of cutting becomes troublesome, they immediately change to a situation more convenient, and more profitable, which they first strip of all its valuable Timbers for Exportation to the French and Dutch Islands. . . . It is therefore for these Reasons humbly submitted to your Lordship's Consideration, whether the renewing the negotiations . . . on the part of the Crown, for the purchase of the proprietorship of the Islands, would not be of the highest advantages, as thereby the rambling Inhabitants must be tied down to their own plantations, which would be secured to them and their Heirs by legal Grants, and would not only help to discourage that abominable Custom of wrecking, and the carrying on an illicit trade, which last is practiced in a high degree with the Dutch, French, and Danish Islands in the West Indies.[6]

The Late-Eighteenth-Century Social Context

As the war with the former American colonies came to an end, a military report in 1783 was intended to assess "the present state of Defences at Providence." It would "report particularly . . . The face & nature of the Country, soil, and produce. State of Cultivation—Number of Inhabitants—of whom composed & how connected."[7] The report includes an enumeration of the categories of inhabitants as of May 1782 on the seven populated islands in the archipelago.

These population statistics for the Bahamas are as interesting for what they do as for what they do not explicitly state. A military officer created this report with an emphasis on the economic potential of the islands. It included a tabulation of taxable persons on each of the seven inhabited islands. It is interesting to note that there were nearly twice as many nontaxable as taxable inhabitants.

One column lists the numbers of those "capable of carrying arms." The officer reported that "the male inhabitants of the Bahama Islands above the age of fifteen, have for many years back been formed into a Militia." Gov. Thomas Shirley had noted some years earlier in a report to the Board of Trade in London that "there is a Poll Tax imposed on all White Males and on all Negro, Mulatto and Indian Men and Women of a certain Age, as a Revenue for the Payment of Officers Salaries, defraying the Expence of holding Assemblies and other Contingent Charges of the Government of these Islands."[8] The tabulation of nontaxables listed in the 1782 table appears to have included white females and all children, regardless of color. The system of taxation reflected a focus on adult white males and all adult blacks as the economic providers. Contemporary sources such as newspaper advertisements, court records, and travel accounts that documented how people made a living indicate that free women of color often worked as domestics, washerwomen, and street vendors to support themselves and their families. Such details provide some information on how free people of color made a living.[9] This kind of information also provides insight into the subculture nonwhites created that paralleled the culture of the wider dominant society.

This population assessment was made in 1782, shortly before Loyalist refugees began arriving in the Bahamas from the former American colonies. Many of these Loyalists had owned plantations in the southern colonies and brought their enslaved workers with them, adding not only to the numbers of African descendants in the Bahamas but also the diversity of places where they had lived. The most heavily populated settlements for blacks and whites were on New Providence, Eleuthera, and tiny Harbour Island, all of which were located in the central region of the archipelago. It was also notable that the population figures fluctuated for Turks Island, at the southern end of the island chain, because its residents were Bermudians who seasonally moved to that island to rake salt.[10]

Population assessment from a Loyalist perspective focused on comparisons between "old" and "new" inhabitants. In 1789, William Wylly published a pamphlet in London extolling the contributions Loyalists made to the Bahamas and detailing the conditions the colonial home government needed to address in this colony to make the transition more amenable for Loyalist migrants.

The influx of Loyalist immigrants had a significant impact on the small colony. Social tensions instigated by the arrival of new migrants served to delineate the array of social groups in the colony. White inhabitants included both "old" and "new" settlers. New Loyalist settlers were wealthier and better educated than the old inhabitants, whom Loyalists disparagingly nicknamed "Conchs." These new settlers wished to and did translate their numerical strength into political power as soon as they could be voted into the Assembly.

Free blacks on New Providence were most heavily impacted by these social changes. Wylly's tabulation of "old" inhabitants suggests that some of them had received land grants to establish plantations on previously un-inhabited or sparsely inhabited islands, such as Andros and Caicos. Since the 1760s, a primary concern for the colonial government had been how to stimulate the economy. The most promising solution seemed to be increasing the amount of land granted for cultivation. Some plantation land grants had been issued in the twenty years prior to the influx of Loyalist immigrants, but with their arrival, the demand for land grants exploded. Though free blacks may not have benefited from land grants, they also participated in this internal migration to other Bahama islands, such as Long Island, where Wylly noted there were 21 "families of colour" in 1788, compared to the one free-born mulatto and one manumitted person who had been reported for this island in 1782.

Other indirect evidence suggests that free blacks were selling their property and were likely relocating to other islands such as Eleuthera. This evidence includes newspaper notices of properties for sale that included wattle-and-daub structures. In the Bahamas, this architectural technique is historically associated with people of African descent (Farnsworth 1999, 100–101). Johann Schoepf, who visited Nassau shortly before Loyalist refugees began arriving in 1783, noted that most of the houses were wooden ([1788] 1911, 263). Since the seventeenth-century Bahamian settlers commonly collected and sold tropical hardwoods, the presumption is that wood was a readily available housing material, even for poor whites and free people of color. Cut stone (blocks of limestone) would have been a more expensive building material, as cutting the solid stone blocks required access to suitable property and intensive manual labor. These building materials were typically used by European settlers, even poor whites. The distinctive construction technique of using wattle and lime plaster would have been recognized as a specifically African-derived building method in the Bahamas. My own family's oral history and archival documentation suggests that my racially mixed Turner ancestors participated in this trend, moving to Eleuthera after being manumitted in Nassau between 1787 and 1828.[11]

A major source of contention for Loyalist migrants to the Bahamas concerned the status of free blacks. Some free blacks and runaway slaves had also migrated to the Bahamas. A Negro Court was established to settle cases in which blacks "either entitled to freedom,—or belonging to persons who are now subjects of the American States were trepanned from the Continent to the Bahama Islands, where they are illegally held in bondage" (Wylly 1789, 22). Though Wylly acknowledged that there were cases of illegal reenslavement, he was still distrustful of free black settlements, stating that "the Town of Nassau is actually overawed by a considerable body of runaway and other Negroes, collected and kept together in the neighbourhood of Government House, and about Fort Charlotte" (ibid.).

The free black settlement south of the Government House property was not formally recognized until the 1820s, when it was named Grant's Town after the governor at the time (Department of Archives, Nassau 1982, 28–30). The area today is also commonly known as "Over the Hill" because of its location immediately south of the ridge that marks the southern boundary of the city of Nassau. Until about 1913, the Government House property extended down the southern slope of this ridge, ending at Cockburn Street.[12] The wall for the Government House property along this street originally served as the northern boundary for the free black settlement that seemed to so anger and frustrate new Loyalist settlers such as Wylly. The status of free blacks was arguably the most contentious issue for Loyalist migrants in the Bahamas.[13] Most free blacks lived on Eleuthera, where it appears that no Loyalists initially moved, and New Providence, where the capital, Nassau, was located. Eleuthera was the next most populous island after New Providence even before the Loyalists arrived.

As Eleuthera is the fifth largest island in the archipelago but had a population of only about 500 in 1782,[14] it is unlikely that Loyalists chose not to move to Eleuthera because of overcrowding or lack of land for settlement. The fact that Loyalist refugees chose not to settle on either Eleuthera or Harbour Island, the sites of the colony's oldest English settlements, suggests instead that there were significant tensions between "old" and "new" inhabitants. On Harbour Island, which is less than one square mile in area, there may not have been any "unclaimed land" to be formally granted as Crown land. However, the same could not be said of Eleuthera, which is over 100 miles long (although it is less than 100 feet wide in places); it is one of the largest islands in the archipelago. As Wylly noted, the basis of wealth was different for the two groups. Property for the Loyalist migrants involved land ownership and control of slave labor. In contrast, property for the "old" Bahamian inhabitants, including free blacks, was more fluid and entailed access to economically viable resources such as tropical hardwoods, salt, fish, and turtles. Thus, "old" settlers needed seaworthy vessels and community agreements about access to these resources rather than ownership title to the property.

This lack of emphasis on landed property ownership would have been affected by the fact that title to property in the Bahamas had remained legally vested in the six lord proprietors from 1670 until the 1780s, when Loyalist migrants arrived. While Gov. Browne cited this situation as a hindrance to the colony's economic development, the unsettled nature of land ownership allowed free blacks, and even slaves to take advantage of this legal uncertainty to claim land for planting.[15] One objective of the 1767 Act for Governing of Negroes, Mulattoes, and Indians was to limit the economic potential of individuals who had been freed (as opposed to free-born individuals). Freed blacks were prohibited from planting cotton, coffee, or indigo (Craton and Saunders 1992, 152–155). This legislation sought to limit the ability of formerly enslaved persons to own land and become socially respected planters.

Even before the arrival of Loyalist migrants, this was a class-based and racially stratified society with a system of economic wealth that was based on access to seemingly unrestricted natural resources. There was less motivation to severely restrict lower-ranked groups such as free people of color than there was in soil-rich colonies with economies based on large-scale cultivation and land ownership. This difference was especially evident in the pattern of property ownership in the town of Nassau in the transition phase of the 1780s, when Loyalist migrants were moving into the Bahamas. A 1788 map of property owners in Nassau shows that about thirty of about 145 landowners in the town were free people of color. On the 1770 map of Nassau, only seven of 120 property owners were nonwhites. By 1800, after Loyalist migrants had become entrenched in the town, the only property owners in Nassau who were free people of color were concentrated on the western edge of the town in an area known as Delancy Town. In the last quarter of the eighteenth century, this neighborhood was named after a free man of color, Stephen Delancy, a successful businessman who lived in the area.

Before the wave of Loyalist migrants moved into Nassau, free people of color owned property around the town, including land east of the governor's mansion on the ridge overlooking the town and in the center of the town, where the new jail was completed in 1799 (Bahamas, Public Records Office 1975, 10). It appears that the only area where nonwhites were restricted from owning property was on the harbor front in the center of the town. The presumption is that because this area provided access to the docks, private property owners in this area exercised some measure of control over commodities entering and being exported from the colony. In short, ownership of harbor-front property in the town was indicative of an individual's level of economic power within the colony. This pattern of ownership remains intact even today. It has been a slow process to convince private dock owners to relocate to the edge of the city to relieve congestion and create a more picturesque harbor profile reflecting the city's current tourist economy.

Despite this apparent façade of social acceptance, the social status for free people of color in the Bahamas was in flux for much of the eighteenth century. Craton and Saunders argue that as the century progressed it became increasingly more difficult to be defined as a free person of color. This was illustrated in a 1756 act "to ascertain who shall not be deemed Mulattoes" that was intended to limit upward mobility for persons of color and reinforce white dominance, not only by reasserting that only whites could be fully free but also by implying that only a strict biological description (rather than economic status or social acceptance) could define a person as "white." The preamble to the act claimed that it was passed because "many good subjects were deprived of doing themselves justice by being deemed Mulattoes." The act stipulated that "all Persons who are above Three Degrees removed in a lineal descent from the Negro Ancestor exclusive shall be deemed white, and shall have all the Privileges and Immunities of His Majesty's White Subjects of these Islands, Provided they are Free, and brought up in the Christian Religion" (Craton and Saunders 1992, 151–152).

Such means of social control were attempts to limit the social mobility of racially mixed individuals. Two wills written in the 1740s show the extent to which racial and social boundaries were blurred. In 1743, John Stead, a white man, died and left his material goods to three female relatives. At least two of these women were married to free men of color. Another example was Benjamin Sims, a mariner, who died about a year after Stead. Sims's estate was worth considerably more than Stead's. His will stipulated that his nine slaves be manumitted on his death. Craton and Saunders suggest that these could have been Sims's common-law wife and their adult children and a grandchild. The executors for Sims's estate were substantial planters and slave owners; one of them had served as acting governor for the colony (Craton and Saunders 1992, 149–150). The cases of Stead and Sims demonstrate the level of social interconnectedness free people of color could attain in the eighteenth-century Bahamas.[16] Craton and Saunders cited these examples to illustrate general improvements in the material condition of Bahamians from the 1720s, when pirates were expelled, to the more comfortable estate listings of the 1740s. The 1750s legislation more clearly delineated who could be considered white. These examples are consistent with the hypothesis that increased material wealth was correlated with increased social control and increased racial distance between whites and all others.

The 1756 legislation made social mobility more difficult for all free blacks in the colony. After the Loyalist migrants arrived and the expectation for a more vibrant economy increased, these racially based social distinctions were scrutinized even more thoroughly. Not surprisingly, free blacks were the social group that was most adversely impacted by the arrival of Loyalist settlers. Census figures and documentation of land ownership suggest that some free blacks moved out of Nassau and resettled in Out Island communities, particularly in Eleuthera and Long Island, after Loyalist settlers came because free blacks then became a focus for Loyalist harassment.[17]

Even the establishment of the Negro Court was insufficient to discourage the new settlers from challenging the rights of free blacks to their freedom. In a confidential dispatch to the Colonial Office, Gov. Dunmore reported the prosecution of a group of Loyalist settlers who had been forcibly entering homes in free black communities in search of alleged runaways. Blacks who were unable to provide credible proof of their freedom, either with some document or with the evidence of a white witness, were being reenslaved.[18]

According to the record of property ownership on the 1788 map of Nassau, the town was not racially segregated, although the highest concentration of nonwhite property owners was on the western edge of the town. By the 1780s, Delancy Town, was predominantly inhabited by socially mobile free people of color (Department of Archives, Nassau, 1982, 1). The fact that this neighborhood was inhabited mainly by free people of color even after Loyalist migrants settled in Nassau suggests that it was figuratively and physically on the fringe of the town's social and economic order.

Less well-to-do blacks established communities beyond the ridge that was Nassau's southern border. These communities were most controversial during the early Loyalist settlement period. Since the basis of property for Loyalist settlers was control of slave labor, they were distrustful of any community of free blacks, believing that such communities provided hiding places for runaway slaves. In his pamphlet, William Wylly described the tension between Loyalist settlers and the colonial administration related to determining the status of some free blacks. Wylly wrote that throughout the Bahamas there was a small group of "people of Colour, either free, or pretending to be so. They are mostly however runaways from the American States" (Wylly 1789, 8).

In this tense environment, it is not surprising that some free blacks chose to leave the urban uncertainty of Nassau and move to the Out Islands,[19] particularly Eleuthera, where Loyalist settlers did not commonly move. Many of the new settlers preferred to live in town and bought whatever property became available. Given the stagnant nature of the colony's economy up to that point, the infusion of cash would have been undeniably attractive to most property owners. Money from the sale of property would have facilitated relocation to another community. Although there is no map later than that of 1788 with as much information on property ownership, it is apparent that by the early nineteenth century there were many fewer Nassau property owners who were free people of color. Those who remained owned property only on the edges of town. They certainly did not own property along Bay Street, the town's main thoroughfare that represented the core of economic power in the colony.

Despite the enthusiasm for large-scale cotton production, by 1800 it was evident that plantation agriculture would not become the dominant economic contributor in the Bahamas. The heyday of cotton production in the Bahamas was the 1780s and 1790s. Responses to a government questionnaire issued in 1800 to prominent planters indicated the major factors they felt contributed most to the decline in production on their plantations. The factors included clearing more land than could be effectively cultivated, not leaving some larger trees to act as windbreaks for crops, infestations of pests such as the chenille bug, the devastating effects of droughts, and cold weather. The overall effect of these factors was to limit soil fertility. Another detail revealed in these responses is that a number of Loyalist planters had already left the colony and many more were planning to leave.[20]

The Colonial Power Structure in the Bahamas

This brief but intense period of American Loyalists' adjustment to the Bahamas served to illustrate the interactions among all the social groups that made up Bahamian colonial society. Apart from the Loyalist migrants, these groups included the earlier population of white settlers, the governor, members of the military, free blacks, and slaves. Interaction among these groups reflected the peculiarities of the social order that developed in the small, marginal colony of the Bahamas.

Because there was less material wealth and education, on average, in the Bahamas than most Loyalist migrants were accustomed to, the "old" settlers found themselves relegated to the less powerful position of lower-status whites. Documentary records only hint at the social tensions between the "old" and "new" white settlers. Other evidence of this social tension can be seen in their patterns of social behavior. Religious affiliation is one such indicator.

The arrival of Loyalist immigrants necessitated the creation of two new parishes of the Anglican Church, one of the two state-supported denominations of the United Kingdom (the other being the Presbyterian Church). St. Matthew's Parish covered the eastern end of Nassau and the eastern end of New Providence Island. St. Patrick's Parish covered the island of Eleuthera but was centered in Governor's Harbour. To accommodate Loyalists of Scottish heritage, St. Andrew's Presbyterian Kirk was centered in the town of Nassau.

The Baptist and Methodist denominations, which functioned independent of government support, were also introduced into the colony during this period. In both cases, the first missionaries to the Bahamas were free people of color who had migrated from the former American colonies. The Methodist Missionary Society had included the Bahamas on its circuit and sent missionaries to these islands since the late eighteenth century. The presence of white missionaries increased the possibility of attracting whites as converts. The majority of white converts to Methodism were in Eleuthera and its cays, members of "old" settler communities. It is likely that group tensions between "old" and "new" settlers affected individual decisions about whether to become (or continue as) Anglican or to become Methodist. It was likely not coincidental that "old" settlers on Eleuthera opted to join the new Methodist denomination rather than remain Anglican, the most common affiliation for Loyalist settlers.

The governor was at the apex of the political and social ladder. His power was based on his appointment as a royal governor and was dependent on the home government and was relatively independent of the power elites in the colonies. The last royal governor of Virginia, John Murray, Earl of Dunmore, was reassigned as governor of the Bahamas in 1787. Although he moved to the Bahamas as part of the Loyalist migration, he did not represent the private interests of that group. Almost as soon as he arrived, he ran afoul of Loyalist planters by issuing a proclamation granting greater legal protection to free blacks.

Disgruntled Loyalist property owners would have to lobby in London to have him recalled. This was one of the motives behind the 1789 publication of William Wylly's pamphlet, the full title of which was *A Short Account of the Bahama Islands, Their Climate, Productions, &c., to Which Are Added, Some Strictures upon Their Relative and Political Situation, the Defects of Their Present Government, &c. &c.* Loyalist lobbying efforts finally resulted in Gov. Dunmore being recalled in 1797 (Williams 1999, 18). This was not only an issue for Lord Dunmore. The most sensitive issue for colonial governors was to reconcile the divergent interests of local elites and those of the home government. Most often these conflicts involved the welfare of enslaved workers or the status of free blacks.

Members of the military were a separate social group. Like the governor, military personnel were assigned their duties from headquarters in London, the Colonial War Office. Their duties were not dictated solely by the requests of colonists; officials in London made appointments based on what they felt were in the best interests of specific colonies. British military forces were heavily engaged during the last quarter of the eighteenth century, especially in the West Indies. Americans invaded the Bahamas during the war between Britain and its American colonies in the 1770s. Then in 1782, the Spanish, encouraged by the American colonists, captured Nassau and held it for a year. The Haitian Revolution and the ensuing Napoleonic Wars in the 1790s prolonged the state of military readiness in the Bahamas.

Fortifications for protecting the colony, especially the administrative center in Nassau, were expanded and upgraded in the 1780s and 1790s. Manning these forts became a critical issue after the 32nd and 47th regiments suffered devastating losses from yellow fever epidemics.[21] Given the context of a constant fear of attack, it was imperative that the colony's fortifications be manned effectively. The decision to staff New Providence's fortifications with black troops was motivated by the poor health record of European troops in the West Indies. The West India Regiments were a permanent corps of black troops commanded by white officers. The British War Office first authorized these special troops in 1795.[22]

Circumstances such as the failure of plantation agriculture, the special requirements for military protection, and the growing abolition movement in Britain all served to mitigate the new social order in which American Loyalist immigrants found themselves in the Bahamas. Colonial directives from London were never developed solely with the interests of the local elite in mind. Free people of color were generally on the fringes of this colonial society, and it was in their best interest to recognize how best to negotiate socially acceptable pathways for themselves. In a marginal colony such as the Bahamas, there could be greater social and economic opportunities for free people of color than would usually be available to free people of color in economically successful colonies. Yet accessing these opportunities involved considerable risks related to restriction of legal rights, the possibility of reenslavement, or even enslavement.

Free Blacks in the Bahamas

The first detachments of the Fifth and Sixth West India Regiments arrived in Nassau on May 4, 1801, from Honduras. It was not well received by the white elite. As Robert Hunt, president of the Legislative Council, who was acting as governor at the time, reported to the Duke of Portland,

> Immediately on the arrival of these Detachments a petition was presented to me by the Speaker of the House of Assembly and other principal inhabitants of Nassau, this being signed by the people at large, with scarcely any exception. . . . . It is not easy, to conceive a more general panic, than the appearance of these Detachments excited the agitation of the public mind could not have been greater had Toussaint himself have come with all his force. I have done every thing in my power to allay the ferment, which I am happy to inform Your Grace has within the last two days considerably subsided. . . . . It is however, I humbly conceive, incumbent on me to state to Your Grace, that the great Numbers of French Negroes and others from different Countries of the very, worst description, who have within these few years found means to introduce themselves into the Colony, afford sufficient ground for apprehinsion [*sic*] and if they should by any artful practices, and they are not deficient in cunning, ingratiate themselves with the Black Troops, the situation of these Islands would be truly alarming.[23]

Clearly these black troops gave rise to fears of the spread of slave rebellion. The reference to "the great Numbers of French Negroes and others . . . of the very worst description" also reflects the ambiguous world blacks inhabited, whether they were enslaved or free, especially those from the former French colony of Saint Domingue. They were most vulnerable in the unsettled and shifting circumstances created by the wars of the late eighteenth and early nineteenth centuries. There was the case for Jean Baptiste, Pierre Louis, Isidora Douis, William, and Saint Yago, slaves who were brought into the Bahamas from Saint Domingue in 1809. William Webb, the searcher of customs for the port of Nassau, reported that he had arrested "certain Negroes appearing to be French Slaves . . . unlawfully imported and brought from the Island of Saint Domingo to the Island of New Providence aforesaid and for sale, as Slaves, in a Certain Spanish Schooner called the San Rafael."[24]

The court allowed four weeks for anyone claiming ownership of these persons to appear. However, "because no Person hath appeared to Claim the aforesaid Negro slaves Jean Baptiste, Pierre Louis, Isidora Douis, William and Saint Yago—Therefore it is considered by the Court that the aforesaid Negro slaves . . . for the Causes aforesaid do remain and be forfeited to our said Lord the King, to be disposed of, according to the form of the status in such case made and provided."[25]

With the enactment of the Slave Trade Act of 1807, the British Parliament legislated that slave ships the Royal Navy seized had to be adjudicated by the nearest British Vice Admiralty Court. If this court ruled that a ship was in violation of the Abolition Act, the vessel and its human cargo were forfeited to the Crown as "prize of war." This forfeiture superseded any prior or future claim of ownership. Though the act stipulated that liberated Africans could not "be sold, disposed of, treated or dealt with as Slaves" by the Crown or its subjects, the law also allowed a colonial official to enlist African recaptives in the military or to assign them as apprentices to private citizens for up to fourteen years (Adderley 2006, 25).[26]

The proceedings of the general court, the Court of Vice Admiralty and all laws passed by the local assembly had to be forwarded to the Secretary of State for the Colonies for final legal approval. When Jean Baptiste, Pierre Louis, Isidora Douis, William, and Saint Yago were brought to the Bahamas, William Vesey Munnings, president of the Legislative Council, was performing the duties of governor until another governor was appointed for the Bahamas. In February 1810, Mr. Munnings sent the required documents to London with a request for a legal opinion about the status of the five slaves condemned to the Crown in 1809. His question was "whether Slaves of all descriptions (the Descendants of Natives of Africa born in foreign Colonies in the West Indies, before or since the passing of the Statute as well as those who are actually Natives of Africa) after Seizure and Condemnation in the Court of Vice Admiralty, are or are not to be disposed of or apprenticed out."[27] This question arose because the local assembly had passed a law in 1808 that stated "that from and after the expiration of six months next after the Publication of this Act, it shall not be lawful for any Person or Persons whatever to sell purchase hire or employ any Slave or Slaves which to his her or their Knowledge did, or now do belong to any subject of the French Government or to any Person or persons residing within any of the Territories, Colonies or Dominions thereof and which

Slave or Slaves, has or have been imported or brought into these Islands since the twelfth day of February one Thousand seven hundred and ninety three, or which shall or may hereafter be brought or shall arrive or be found within these Islands from the Island of Saint Domingo or any other French Colony Whatsoever."[28]

The act the colonial assembly passed could not supersede the British Parliament's 1807 act abolishing the slave trade. Mr. Munnings did not receive the legal opinion he had requested until October 1811, when the Earl of Liverpool, the next secretary of state for the colonies, wrote to him. The earl wrote that "the Law Officers of the Crown are of Opinion that in whatever manner the provisions of that Act may apply to the present Case, that the importation of the Negroes in question was at all events illegal under the Navigation Acts if not under the 47 Geo.3.C.36. Under these circumstances the Negroes ought to be treated as free & with the exception of the one who is a Native of Africa & who appears to have been apprenticed out under the act they ought to be set at Liberty."[29]

This was the first case from the Bahamas in which the provisions of the 1807 Slave Trade Act were applied to creole blacks (those born in the Americas). Although the five persons named in the case were set free because they were born in the Americas, a sixth individual who was also a part of this case remained as an apprentice because this person had been born in Africa. As an apprentice this person was required to serve for at least seven years. In another case from the Vice Admiralty Court, Catharine Richardson, a free woman of color, had traveled to Nassau in June 1809 from New York in the company of a white man. The man left her in Nassau because he had sold her as a slave. In the Vice Admiralty Court she was "Condemned for want of Claim; discharged being a Creole."[30]

Most illegal slaving ships were intercepted near the West African coast so the majority of these African recaptives, or liberated Africans, were resettled in Sierra Leone. Many others were resettled in the British Caribbean in the period 1807–1834. During this period the Bahamas received most of these "new Negroes from Africa" (Adderley 2006, 2). The location of the archipelago on shipping lanes near the thriving slave markets of Cuba and the southern United States meant that the Bahamas were close to the heaviest slaving traffic in the western Caribbean. From 1807 to 1860, over 6,000 liberated Africans were resettled in the Bahamas. Almost one-third of these had arrived by 1834 (ibid., 241–242). From 1834 onward, the larger British Caribbean territories of Jamaica, Trinidad, and Guiana received thousands of African recaptives as indentured workers along with recruits from India, China, and Madeira. These populations replenished a plantation labor force that was decimated after emancipation (ibid., 7–8).

Liberated Africans were also the main source of recruits for the members of the West India Regiments. To protect their status after they were discharged, the 1807 Mutiny Act declared that "all Negroes . . . Serving in His Majesty's Forces, shall be, and be deemed and taken to be free, to all Intents and for all purposes whatever" (Buckley 1979, 78–79). The inclusion of a free African population had major implications for Bahamian society. The first significant group of liberated Africans to be resettled in the Bahamas arrived in 1811, when more than 400 men, women, and children were brought to these islands. They were parceled out to individual planters and merchants, who were supposed to ensure that they were trained in some trade. William Wylly, a prominent Loyalist planter, was assigned four liberated African men in 1811. They lived and worked on his largest plantation, Clifton, at the western end of New Providence (Wilkie and Farnsworth 2005, 60–61). Archaeological investigations suggest that at least one of these men was a private in the Sixth West India Regiment (Wilkie and Farnsworth 2005, 292). Timothy Cox, a free colored ship carpenter, was also assigned a liberated African apprentice (H. Johnson 1996, 27, 31).

Planters presented two petitions complaining about the addition of more free blacks to the colony's population. In the second petition, the complainants admitted that these new immigrants brought potential economic benefit to the colony's labor force (Adderley 2006, 32–35). In addition, this group of settlers made a distinctive contribution to the character of Bahamian society. The settlement of liberated Africans and other free black immigrants served to illustrate the interplay between official colonial policies and local social custom.

In 1825 Gov. Lewis Grant revised the way in which liberated Africans were to serve their apprenticeships. They were no longer to be assigned to individual employers but were to live in settlements created especially for the resettlement of liberated Africans.[31] The collector of customs, in 1825, was authorized to purchase 400 acres of land in the southwestern interior of New Providence to be apportioned equally to each African resident.

The village, initially called Headquarters, was later named Carmichael after pro-abolition governor James Carmichael Smyth (Settlements 1982, 22). The residents of Carmichael grew fruits and vegetables that they sold at the public market in Nassau. Since this settlement was some ten miles away from Nassau, many residents chose to relocate closer to town, settling in the region called Over the Hill (Williams [1979] 1991, 7). There is evidence that free blacks settled this area beginning in the eighteenth century. The only road that traversed the island, Baillou (Blue) Hill Road, was put through here in 1795. This road provided easier access from the island's interior into town and the public market. After this influx of new residents into the Over-the-Hill area (the common name for the neighborhood even today) the surveyor-general officially laid out a settlement, Grant's Town, that was named for Gov. Lewis Grant (Department of Archives, Nassau, 1982, 28).

Liberated Africans understood that their status allowed them to be totally free when they completed their apprenticeships. Their legal status as liberated Africans allowed them a ranking that was higher than that of enslaved persons. Though the British colonial administration advocated policies to protect African recaptives, there was still a general belief that they were culturally and, by extension, intellectually inferior. This attitude was most apparent in a comment by Alexander Murray, a former collector of customs in the Bahamas, that "some hundreds of savages from Africa have been turned loose amongst them—unshackled from the restraints which the Laws imposed on the slaves" (Adderley 2006, epigraph). The placement of liberated African settlements at some distance from Nassau suggests a preference for keeping this group of free blacks apart from respectable social life. None of these villages were closer than ten miles from Nassau. Since the residents would have had to walk to town, usually along trails, this meant a round trip of at least half a day.

Despite such hindrances, liberated Africans made an indelible impact on Bahamian society. Documentary evidence from New Providence suggests that liberated Africans preferred to live in ethnic neighborhoods in all of their settlements (Adderley 2006, 118–125; Eneas [1976] 1988, 28–29, 35–36). Theoretically these Africans did not have to relinquish their cultural identity to the extent that enslaved Africans had to do. Evidence of cases where they relinquished their inherited African cultural traditions in exchange for European-style cultural behavior suggests deliberate social

choice. One element of this research was to investigate what factors contributed to when and why African-descended people made these cultural
decisions.

Some of these individuals were able to make the considerable transition
from being considered a savage African to being regarded as a "civilized"
British subject. This was the case of Monday Ranger, who would have come
to the Bahamas as a liberated African. The inscription on his headstone
stated that he was born in Lagos, Nigeria, in 1815, after the passage of 1807
Slave Trade Act. A granite headstone marks his gravesite in the southwest
quadrant of Nassau's historic Western Cemetery. This cemetery was originally reserved for whites, but in 1833, Gov. B. T. Balfour told Anglican clergy
"that for the future no distinction of burial ground [should] be made between the white and Coloured man[.] Let us at least have the consolation
of feeling that distinctions of pride are lost in the grave."[32] Thus, by the
time Monday Ranger died in 1902, the Western Cemetery had long been
an integrated but high-status burial space.

The case of a free black French immigrant family illustrates the process
of social inclusion that enabled a few nonwhite families to be accepted in
privileged social circles. Hester Argo and her young son, Stephen Dillet,
relocated to the Bahamas from "Hayti" around 1803 (Thompson 2002, 129).
Stephen Dillet's first child, Edwin Stephen, was born August 19, 1818. By
1822 he was married to Charlotte and their first child, Thomas William
Henry, was born September 29, 1823. The father, Stephen Dillet, is listed as
a "coloured tailor" with a shop located just a block south of Bay Street, the
main street through the town of Nassau. Socially Mr. Dillet had attained as
high a social status possible for a free man of color at this time.[33]

Stephen Dillet was among eleven free blacks who formed the Committee of Free Persons of Colour in New Providence Island. The aim of
the committee was to lobby for the repeal of discriminatory legislation
passed by the Loyalist-dominated Assembly in the 1790s and early 1800s.
Such legislation included the 1802 Act to Suspend an Act to Ascertain
Who Shall Not Be Deemed Mulattoes (Johnson 2001, 35; McWeeney 2002,
21). This act nullified the provisions of a 1756 act that specified who could
qualify to be a white person. The objective of the 1802 legislation was to
restrict the social mobility of nonwhites even more than the 1756 act had.

In spite of the rhetoric of this 1802 act, the examples cited demonstrate
that the social reality continued to resemble the less stringently racialized

social order that had characterized Bahamian society before the Loyalists arrived. Nevertheless, free coloreds would have been most adversely affected by the new social thinking American Loyalists introduced. Although in Britain, members of a pro-abolition movement promoted the welfare of enslaved laborers, free people of color had no such advocates.

In the period 1823–1833, the Bahamian Parliament passed the Amelioration Acts because of pressure from the British government. These acts reaffirmed the provisions of a 1797 act that stipulated that owners had to provide food and clothing for enslaved workers, but they went further than that. An 1824 act protected all slaves against physical abuse, permitted slaves to enjoy certain holidays, legalized slave marriages, and prohibited the separation of slave families. An 1826 law made it legal for slaves to own property and allowed slaves to give evidence in civil and criminal cases, with some restrictions. Slave evidence was inadmissible in cases involving another slave's claim to freedom, and slaves could not give evidence against a white person in death penalty cases. Only creole Christian slaves who had been in the Bahamas at least five years could give evidence (W. B. Johnson 1996, 25–26).

Laws affecting free people of color were not as progressive. Gov. Carmichael Smyth disallowed the 1827 Jury Act because it denied free people of color the right to serve as jurors. A revised Jury Bill in 1833 set juror qualifications so high that few people of color could qualify (Williams 1999, 22–23). Such legislation probably was the catalyst for the formation of the Committee of Free Persons of Colour in New Providence Island. The efforts of committee members appear to have had some impact, as free men of color were given the right to vote by 1830. In 1834, the first free coloreds were elected to the Assembly: Stephen Dillet and John Patrick Dean for New Providence and Edward P. Laroda for Exuma. Laroda was one of several free men of color who had petitioned the House of Assembly beginning in November 1828 for the right to vote (Johnson 2001, 35).[34] Voting privileges at this time were given to males at least 21 years of age who owned property "over and above what will satisfy and clear all judgments and mortgages ... of the value of two hundred pounds, lawful money of the said islands; or who shall be proprietors of fifty acres of land under cultivation, within these islands, free from all legal incumbrances"[35]

By the time the Emancipation Act became effective on August 1, 1834, several groups of blacks had been allowed to settle in the Bahamas as free people. One such group was the Black Seminoles, who had moved to the

Bahamas from Florida because of General Andrew Jackson's aggressive campaign against native groups who sought refuge there. Seminole chiefs had visited the governor of the Bahamas twice (Kenadgie in 1819 and Hoopay in 1821) to request Britain's help for their people against the Americans. The Seminoles had sided with the British in the War of 1812 and assumed that the British would provide them reciprocal assistance (Wood 1987, 4–7; Howard 2002, 30–31). On both occasions the governors were cordial but offered no substantial help. In the early 1820s a group of Black Seminoles (blacks who had found refuge among the Seminoles and those of mixed African and native ancestry) paid a white Bahamian wrecker, James Mott, to transport them to the Bahamas aboard his vessel named *Sheerwater*. Mott apparently landed the group on the unoccupied west coast of Andros Island, where they established a settlement. Another community settled in the tiny Berry Islands but the location of this settlement is unknown (Howard 2002).

In 1828 Winer Bethell, the searcher of customs, reported to the governor that he had seized "97 foreign negro slaves at Andros." Mr. Bethell assumed that these people were slaves illegally brought in from Florida and that smugglers were waiting for an opportune time to take them to Cuba to be sold. According to persons in the group, they had either escaped enslavement on their own or had been captured by British ships patrolling the U.S. coast. Most still had discharge papers to verify that they had fought with the British during the Battle of New Orleans in 1815. Those who chose to remain in Florida felt so pressured by U.S. authorities that in 1821 "they applied to and persuaded the owners of some Bahama fishing vessels . . . to take them on board and to carry them to any island in the British Crown" (Wood 1987, 12; see also Howard 2002, 31–32).

Their settlement at Red Bays is the only one on the west coast of Andros. This sparsely populated island was the largest island in the archipelago. Whoever helped these 97 people get to Andros likely estimated that they would remain undetected and unmolested for some time. Gov. James Carmichael Smyth explained to Lord Bathurst in 1831 that in the seven years these people had lived on Andros, none had been carried off to Cuba and sold into slavery. He concluded that "these people have never been considered in this Colony as slaves and their names have never been entered on the slave registry. . . . If the name is not in the Registry the state of slavery cannot be established."

Gov. Smyth's only recommendation was to request a stipendiary clergyman who could visit islands where there was no church. The likely presumption was that the Church of England would have a moderating and civilizing influence on the community. The residents of Red Bays were grateful enough to Gov. Carmichael Smyth that they were among the free people of color who submitted petitions expressing regret when he was removed as governor in 1832 (Wood 1987, 13).

In addition to these Black Seminole settlers, there was another category of free Blacks from America who were settled in the Bahamas. In 1825, Britain's Colonial Office ruled that slaves brought to the Bahamas from outside the British West Indies were to be manumitted. Over the next forty years, more than 350 enslaved Americans were freed in the Bahamas under this ruling (Marotti 2004, 5). Most had been shipwrecked in Bahamian waters.

Apparently communities of enslaved laborers in the United States heard of the British law and the freed slaves in the Bahamas. In at least one case there is evidence that such knowledge led to a bid for freedom. Ships sailing south along the east coast of the United States routinely passed through channels in the northern Bahamas to get around the prevailing north-flowing currents in the Gulf of Florida. One of these was the *Creole*, which sailed from Hampton Roads, Virginia, in October 1841, en route to New Orleans. On board were 135 enslaved persons who were to be sold in New Orleans. They were likely aware that in the previous year another Hampton Roads vessel, the *Hermosa*, had run aground in the Abaco Islands in the northern Bahamas. Bahamian wreckers had rescued everyone on board and taken them to Nassau, where the enslaved persons were freed (Eden 2000, 14).

Once the *Creole* was in Bahamian waters near the Abaco Islands, a group of nineteen slaves overpowered the crew and took charge of the ship. During the takeover, an agent was killed and the captain and a crewman were injured. According to U.S. documents, which are based on the testimony of the crew in the ensuing inquiry, these nineteen men asked to be taken to Liberia. However, given their probable knowledge that U.S. slaves could be freed by British officials in Nassau, it is more likely they demanded to be taken to Nassau. The nineteen rebels killed or injured the slave agent, the captain, and the first mate, then they coerced the rest of the crew to sail for Nassau. Once in Nassau, the network of recently emancipated blacks thwarted the plans of the white crew and the U.S. consul to sneak the ship away with the slaves on board. While the nineteen involved in the takeover were held in prison, the remaining 116 slaves were allowed to go free. (Three mulatto women chose to return to the United States with their two children [Eden 2000, 16].) Meanwhile, the governor sought legal advice from London about whether the nineteen insurrectionists could be charged with piracy and murder. They also sought advice on how to handle the U.S. consul's charge that the other 116 slaves were illegally allowed to go free. The law officers for the Crown ruled that the intent of the nineteen slaves was not piracy but to gain their freedom. They also concluded that these men could not be charged for murder in a British court because the incident occurred on a foreign vessel and did not involve any British subjects.[36] By the time these decisions reached Nassau, one of the nineteen participants had died of his injuries, so only eighteen men received the freedom they coveted.

Such cases detail some of the complexities of the small but extremely varied free black population in the Bahamas immediately before and shortly after full emancipation. As a concession to West Indian planters, the 1833 Emancipation Act provided for a gradual transition to full emancipation by means of an apprenticeship period. Initially this apprenticeship phase was to be six years for praedial (field) slaves, and four years for non-praedial slaves. In 1838, all apprenticeships were considered completed after four years. The Bahamas did not experience the unrest that came with emancipation in some West Indian colonies. A major reason was that Bahamian apprentices generally had access to land. While many former slaves became squatters on unused Crown lands, on some Out Islands they became tenant farmers in a crop-sharing system (H. Johnson 1996, 84–97; Saunders 1993, 63). However, after full emancipation in 1838, former slaves were able to freely relocate wherever they chose.

When Emancipation Came

There is evidence that there was extensive internal migration in the Bahamas in the 1840s. Andros had a major population influx. A likely motivation was not simply access to available land but also the opportunity to participate in sponging, one of the colony's fastest growing industries. The most extensive sponge beds in the archipelago were located in the shallows off the west coast of Andros. In the same way that former slaves created a peasant class in islands such as Jamaica (Higman 1984, 386–390; Craton and Saunders 2000, 53), emancipated laborers in the Bahamas developed a large seafaring work force. During the period of slavery, the Bahamas had the highest percentage of enslaved mariners in the British West Indies (Higman 1984, 48). On the eve of emancipation, skilled mariners were being bought, or otherwise traded, apparently in efforts by Bahamian slave owners to establish labor contracts that would extend well beyond the interim apprenticeship period (Turner 2007, 6).

Though Bahamians of African descent were able to build new lives for themselves as free people after emancipation, the critical issues at this time concerned the quality of their new lives. After emancipation, the Anglican Church set up chapels on New Providence in Grant's Town and Delancy Town. The Church also supported schools for these communities. Anglican churches and schools were also built in the liberated African settlements at Gambier, Adelaide, and Carmichael. Methodist and Baptist missionaries were more active in Out Island communities. The British colonial administration believed that religious services and religious teaching would act as socially moderating forces on communicants. The schools provided a basic elementary education. Education beyond this level was not readily available to most Bahamians, be they black or white.

Many formerly enslaved Bahamians became landowners by purchasing, leasing, renting, or simply squatting on available land. They understood the significance of landownership as a basic economic resource, but landownership could also have other benefits. Only men who owned a certain amount of property could vote in parliamentary elections. Control of and access to real property assets could confer social and economic power on an individual, but that power was proportional to the assessed value of his property. Most Bahamian property owners faced several issues that could nullify their political power as property owners. Some did not own enough property to qualify to vote, while others were controlled by wealthy businessmen to whom they were indebted. In a voting system that was not by secret ballot, they were obliged to vote for candidates their creditors supported.

The Civil Disabilities Act of 1833 gave free blacks the same legal privileges as whites but excluded African-born individuals (Johnson 2006, 112). In the post-emancipation British Empire, former slaves lost some of the protections they had had as slaves in a British colony. The vigilance of abolitionists ended with the implementation of full emancipation in 1838. This left the masses of former slaves at the mercy of local white elites. British colonial officials were generally of the opinion that religious instruction and basic education provided adequate social protection for the African-descended masses. Similar assumptions regarding the role of organized religion and basic education operated in the social hierarchy of contemporary Britain (Powles [1888] 1996, 43–54; Price 1999, 296–302; Johnson 2006, 6–8; Craton and Saunders 2000, 17–20; Adderley 2006, 12–13).

The truck and credit systems became prevalent in the post-emancipation economy. Workers were paid in kind, or truck. Historian Howard Johnson attributes the pattern of substituting payment in truck for cash wages to the lack of capital available to Bahamian planters even before emancipation. Initially the payment of wages in kind addressed an economic reality in this cash-poor colony. This became the usual payment method in most industries and ensured that Nassau merchants could control local labor (H. Johnson 1996, 88–89; Saunders 1993, 65). Louis D. Powles, a stipendiary magistrate in the Bahamas in the 1880s, described the truck system:

> The principal industries of the colony are the sponge and turtle fisheries, and the cultivation of pineapples. Through the truck system the benefit derived from these sources by the working man is not only reduced to a minimum, but he is virtually kept in bondage to his employer. The sponger and turtler are the greatest sufferers, because they are kept under seaman's articles all the time. . . . He applies to the owner of a craft engaged in the sponge or turtle fisheries, generally in the two combined, to go on a fishing voyage. He is not to be paid by wages, but to receive a share of the profits of the take, thus being theoretically in partnership with his owner. At once comes into play the infernal machine, which grinds him down and keeps him a slave for years and years—often for life. His employer invariably keeps, or is in private partnership with some one else who keeps, a store, which exists principally for the purposes of robbing the employé. (Powles [1888] 1996, 44)

Powles had been appointed stipendiary magistrate of the Bahamas in July 1886 at the governor's insistence. The post replaced resident justices, all of whom Gov. Blake considered to be incompetent and inefficient. Locals resented that this well-paid post was given to an Englishman. As stipendiary magistrate, Powles was expected to make quarterly visits to every island in addition to serving in Nassau. Powles admitted that he came to the Bahamas with a low opinion of blacks, but he soon noticed the unequal administration of justice for blacks and whites. Less than a year after his appointment, Gov. Blake advised Powles to take three months' leave on half pay, after which he was to resign. Powles had so angered Nassau's white elites that they lobbied to have him reassigned outside the Bahamas. The final blow came after Powles convicted a prominent Nassau gentleman of striking his black housemaid (Powles [1888] 1996, 55–57; Themistocleous 1997, 19–20). On his return to London, Powles published his observations of his time in the Bahamas. Because his portrayal of life in the Bahamas was very negative, the book was banned from the colony when it was first published (Williams 1999, 48). Nevertheless, this work is the most comprehensive contemporary account of Bahamian life in the late nineteenth century.

Until the late nineteenth century, after slavery was abolished in the United States and Cuba, black Bahamians had few options for wage-earning employment. While white Bahamians could migrate to the United States, free blacks were not welcome (Whidden 1997, 32; Johnson 2006, 126–127).[37] In the 1850s, the British government warned black Bahamians against traveling to the United States or Cuba because a number of Bahamians had been kidnapped and sold into slavery (Johnson 2006, 60–65; Tinker 2011, 34; Williams 1999, 29). Once emancipation in these countries eliminated these restrictions, Bahamians of any color could take advantage of wage-earning opportunities around the region.

Searching for Work Outside the Bahamas

Beginning in the 1880s, Bahamian laborers from islands along shipping channels in the southern Bahamas were contracted to work aboard ships sailing to Cuba, Haiti, and Panama. In the 1890s, several hundred people emigrated to the United States from the Abaco Islands, Harbour Island, and Bimini. This spate of emigration to the United States, especially to Florida, continued into the first two decades of the twentieth century. Bahamians were employed to drain the Everglades in southern Florida and in agricultural labor throughout the United States, particularly during the two world wars (Department of Archives, Nassau 1986, 17–19; Department of Archives, Nassau 1987, 35).

The arrival of Greek immigrants in the 1880s to participate in the sponge industry helped displace small boat owners, most of whom belonged to the colored middle class. Both whites and blacks initially saw the Greeks as unwanted competitors. A group of black and white sponge-boat owners petitioned the governor to protest the arrival of this new group. Some Greeks left, but those who stayed were soon accepted into the white elite merchant class because after a time Nassau's merchants realized the value of this new group's international marketing networks. This alliance between white Nassau merchants and Greek immigrants effectively eliminated any small Bahamian sponge dealers, a number of whom were "coloured" Bahamians. By the twentieth century, the Bahamas was one of the world's largest producers of sea sponges (Bahamas, Public Records Office 1974, 21).

Beginning in the 1870s, more and more black Bahamians began seeking wage-earning opportunities in the United States, first in Florida and later in New York City. The usual migration pattern was to work in the United States for about five to eight months to earn some money before returning home for several months and then repeating this process. This continuous flow back and forth of Bahamian migrant workers was significantly curtailed by the restrictions of the 1924 Immigration Act. However, the impact of this act was not as severe in the Bahamas as it could have been. Bahamians of all colors made a comfortable living smuggling liquor into the United States during the prohibition era. When prohibition was repealed in the United States in 1933, Bahamians began feeling the effects of the Great Depression more directly. In 1942, shortly after the United States entered World War II, the U.S. and British governments signed an agreement to allow persons from British West Indian territories to be contracted as agricultural guest workers. Under this agreement, known locally as "The Contract" or "The Project," thousands of Bahamians, particularly young men, worked as farm laborers from Florida to Minnesota. They did so from 1943 until the early 1960s, when more employment opportunities became available at home.

Summing It All Up

From the early days of British settlement in the West Indies, the economy of its colonies depended on the exploitation of unfree labor. As a marginal British colony, the Bahamas did not have a highly profitable economy until well into the twentieth century. From the mid-seventeenth century to the late eighteenth century, this casual economic environment fostered a more relaxed social order that maintained a fairly fluid distinction between European and non-European inhabitants. The plantation economy that Loyalist immigrants spearheaded beginning in the 1780s produced a heightened desire to determine who should have access to social, legal, and political privileges.

However, the demands of the local white elite were moderated by a number of factors. Their interests were often at odds with the aims of British colonial policies and with special interest lobbies such as Christian missionaries and abolitionists. The result was a compromise between the competing interests of local elites and the British government. This atmosphere was generally supportive of all free blacks, both creole and African born. By the late 1820s, the last legal restriction for free persons of color was the right to vote. In 1833, the Bahamian parliament granted free men of color voting rights. After that, the greatest differentiation among people of color was based on economic resources, a prime determining factor for distinctions of social class. The social and economic distinctions that were the most important means of categorizing people in Britain were exported to Britain's colonial territories such as the Bahamas. In the United States, in contrast, race was used as the primary way of categorizing people of African descent. Britain did not have to confront issues of race until after World War II, when people from the colonies began migrating to the United Kingdom in search of greater opportunities. As Jamaican comedian Louise Bennett phrased it, "We were colonizin' England in reverse."

The post-emancipation period presented new challenges for formerly enslaved Bahamians since all of the protective legislation and colonial oversight the abolitionist movement had promoted ended with full emancipation in 1838. As early as the 1820s, migration to the United States was an easy option for white Bahamians, but this was not a viable option for blacks until the late nineteenth century. Lack of economic options at home made most black Bahamians more vulnerable to abuse than they had been during enslavement. For the masses of black Bahamians, the strategy of transitory migration served as the major release from the limited opportunities available in the colony. This was the case from the late nineteenth century until the mid-twentieth century, when a wider range of opportunities became available as new economic sectors were developed in the Bahamas.

2

African Influence on Eighteenth- and Nineteenth-Century Cemeteries

What good will it be for someone to gain the whole world, yet forfeit
their soul? Or what can anyone give in exchange for their soul?

Matthew 16:26, New International Version

W. E. B. Du Bois's metaphor of the veil portrays people of African descent
as actively moving between two culturally distinct spheres. This metaphor
implies that African-descended people made conscious cultural decisions
about the ways they structured their lives. The world within the veil is
an African-derived cultural perspective; the world outside the veil is a
European-derived world view that is evident in control of the wider society. In this dual world, African-descended people had three basic options:

Maintain a predominantly African-derived lifestyle with limited
    or no contact with a broader social order
Move continuously between two very different worlds
Decide to function solely in the world of the dominant social order

These three options are all aspects of how the creolization process operated
historically for people in the African Atlantic Diaspora. Creolization can
refer to mixing or it can be what Jamaican historian Kamau Brathwaite
termed "negative creolization"—a refusal to adopt European-oriented materials and practices in areas of life people consider to be the most important (Brathwaite 1977, 54–55). I quoted the Bible verse in the epigraph to
this chapter to convey the gravity of any decisions about whether to give up
inherited cultural practices, which are so important for cultural and group

identity, or to embrace new behaviors and ideas for recrafting a cultural identity. It is this internal personal debate that is brought to the fore with Du Bois's concept of dual consciousness.

Though cultural change happens over time within every cultural group, because of the circumstances under which Africans became immigrants in the Americas there has been a debate about the processes by which Africans in the Americas made cultural transformations. In the historically racialized societies of the Americas, cultural transformations had major implications for a person's racial and broader social identity. Scholars of African descent debated these issues, beginning in the nineteenth century with Frederick Douglass ([1854] 1950) and Anténor Firmin ([1885] 2002). Douglass, Firmin, and Du Bois ([1903] 1989) made the case for an interpretation that considered the perspective of African-descended people in the development of an African-influenced cultural heritage. Even though ideas on race evolved considerably throughout the twentieth century, too often scholars in archaeology of African descent sometimes still approach the interpretation of African-derived cultural heritage in the Americas with the assumption that this cultural heritage was based on a European cultural framework. I use Du Bois's concept of double consciousness to highlight the subtle balance that is achieved by interpreting the cultural placement of European materials in an African-derived cultural framework. Archaeologists have recognized that Africans in the Diaspora used European-made objects but imbued them with African-derived cultural meaning. However, at times this cultural meaning can be so closely held in a cultural group that opportunities to discuss it and thereby recognize it do not readily become available. In the Bahamas, this is the case with cemeteries and African-derived folk beliefs about the power of cemetery spaces.

Over time, no matter what choice a person made about his or her cultural practices, the decision would impact the identity of that person and likely would be passed on to their immediate descendants. Carter Woodson made the following statement about a perception of African cultural heritage that was widespread among people of African descent:

> Negroes themselves accept as a compliment the theory of a complete break with Africa, for above all things they do not care to be known as resembling in any way these "terrible Africans." On the other hand, the whites prate considerably about what they have preserved of the ancient cultures of the "Teutons" or "Anglo-Saxons," emphasizing es-

pecially the good and saying nothing about the undesirable practices. If you tell a white man that his institution of lynching is the result of the custom of raising the "hue and cry" among his tribal ancestors in Germany or that his custom of dealing unceremoniously with both foreigners and Negro citizens regardless of statutory prohibition is the vestigial harking back to the Teuton's practice of the "personality of the law," he becomes enraged. And so do Negroes when you inform them that their religious practices differ from those of their white neighbors chiefly to the extent that they have combined the European with the African superstition. These differences, of course, render the Negroes undesirable to those otherwise religious-minded. The Jews boldly adhere to their old practices while the Negroes, who enjoy their old customs just as much, are ashamed of them because they are not popular among "Teutons." (Woodson 1937, 367)

This attitude remained common until the mid-twentieth century. The implication of this view is that for people of African descent who aspired to any kind of social mobility, it was not in their interest to publicly exhibit any cultural behavior that could be deemed African. Those who did so were viewed as unsophisticated and uncivilized.

Archaeological evidence of the process of change and continuity is present in St. Matthew's Northern Burial Ground. The burial ground is a small site, and remains from the earlier cultural surface are evident within 20 centimeters below the current ground surface. This area was extensively disturbed sometime after the cemetery was closed in the early twentieth century. The cemetery represents the world view of an urban black Bahamian population from the eighteenth to early twentieth centuries. In the Bahamas, as in most societies, the way burial places are cared for involves a conservative approach to cultural practices in order to treat the dead with respect, so cemeteries are optimal sites for studying cultural practices over time. Cemeteries also provide clues to individuals' lives that can be found through bioarchaeological research on their remains. Since this was not a sealed archaeological context, any interpretation of the population and the associated cultural activity in the Northern Burial Ground had to be general. Because destruction of the original site context also involved removal of human skeletal remains, the research design did not focus on skeletal analysis because it would not be possible to identify individual burials. Additionally, the excavated sample of human remains is very small (a minimum number of five individuals) and is really a sample from random excavation rather than a sample that is representative of the historical community. Thus, this sample could be used only to pose questions that any skeletal pathologies might suggest about a broader population.

Even though this site was disturbed, the possibility remained of investigating aspects of the original cultural landscape archaeologically. In only a few cases have archaeologists taken note of culturally significant aspects of the landscape that may be considered as being drawn from an African cultural heritage (Blakey 2001; Armstrong and Fleischman 2003; Lenik 2005; Perry, Howson, and Bianca 2009; Delle and Fellows 2014). This site afforded an opportunity to examine such a cultural landscape. I define "cultural landscape" as the accumulation of culturally meaningful features that a group has invested in a specific site over time. As Angèle Smith has noted, "Landscapes are made by the people that engage with them, and in making landscapes, the people themselves are made: their sense of place, belonging, and their social identity is constructed alongside the construction of the landscape" (Smith 2008, 14; see also Bender, Hamilton, and Tilley 2005, 80–82; Chenoweth 2009, 320–321).

I used cultural and contemporary information from several other cemeteries as a basis of comparison with the Northern Burial Ground. Bethlehem cemetery, another urban cemetery for blacks dates to the late eighteenth century and is located on the western edge (the other side) of Nassau. I also considered evidence I gathered from the public cemetery in Cockburn Town, the administrative capital of San Salvador Island, which dates back to at least the mid-nineteenth century. On Crooked Island, in the south-central region of the archipelago, I surveyed public cemeteries for six settlements. I also considered evidence from elsewhere in the Caribbean, including excavations and studies in historically black cemeteries at Pierhead and Fontabelle cemeteries in Bridgetown, Barbados (Farmer, Smith, and Watson 2005); St. John, in the U.S. Virgin Islands (Blouet 2014); and Montserrat. In the United States, I looked at evidence from black cemeteries in Virginia (Fesler 2004), Philadelphia (McCarthy 2006), and New York City (Perry, Howson, and Bianca 2009). Taken together, the evidence from these sites build the case that landscape features in the Northern Burial Ground should be interpreted as influenced by cultural behavior from West and Central Africa. Additional support for this position comes from the recognition that cemeteries and burial practices constitute one of the strongest domains of what Herskovits (1941) called "cultural focus"; that is, domains of such importance to practitioners that they carry forward traditions that may have become less important in other domains. Documentation in the United States by folklorists, art historians, and cultural anthropologists strengthens Herskovits's claim and has made cemeteries some of the most commonly researched sites of African continuities (Glave 1891; Ingersoll 1892; Parsons 1918; Puckett 1926; Cohen 1958; Thompson and Cornet 1981; Thompson 1984; Sobel 1988; Fenn 1989; Nichols 1989; Vlach 1991; Nigh 1997).

Developing the Concept of an African-Influenced Landscape

Until the rediscovery of the African Burial Ground in New York City, archaeologists investigating cemetery sites had focused mainly on forensic details gathered from excavated skeletal remains. However, the African Burial Ground became a landmark site that demonstrated how archaeologists can engage interested communities in identifying research issues and developing an interpretation that is informed by a group's social and cultural history of the site (McCarthy 1996; LaRoche and Blakey 1997; Patten 1997; Epperson 2004). While archaeologists had previously focused on what was in the grave shaft, the descendant community's desire to understand more about who these individuals were and how they lived extended the archaeological context to include the entire cemetery landscape and the history of Africans and slavery in New York City.

In a similar vein, I see the historical developments in Nassau and the Bahamas as essential for interpreting the Northern Burial Ground. This approach does not assume that because the cemetery was used by a group with limited social power, features on the landscape followed patterns set by the wider society. The research team for the African Burial Ground project responded to the black community's interest in the African origins of persons buried there by interpreting grave goods, personal adornment, spatial orientation of the graves, and the diversity of the African cultural traditions represented, which offered clues to the specific regions on the continent the deceased represented. Because the Northern Burial Ground was disturbed and only a small portion was excavated, less of this information was available from this site. However, much can still be learned when this site is placed in a broad historical and cultural context.

It was important to establish, as much as possible, what cemetery landscapes tell us about where, when, how, and if African-descended people in the Bahamas maintained a distinctive African-influenced cultural identity. Once this is recognized, it is possible to identify if and how these cultural representations changed over time. To simply label such behavior as creolization or to assume that African influences remained static instead of changing in tandem with changes in the larger society is to overlook the myriad nuances that could help us understand the deliberate cultural decisions that people made to either maintain or change specific cultural behavior and to examine possible interpretations of why these decisions were being made.

On Crooked Island, in the south-central Bahamas (about 250 miles [410 kilometers] from Nassau), even into the early years of this century burials were adorned with personal utensils of the deceased and some plant or tree was planted at the head of the grave. According to folklorists, cultural anthropologists, and cemetery preservationists, these culturally constructed landscape features are aspects of a distinct, African-derived cemetery landscape that differs significantly from their Europeanized counterparts. Features of African-derived cemetery landscapes include not only personal utensils and plantings but also a location close to a body of water and faunal remains that suggest either feasting or animal sacrifices on behalf of the spirits of deceased relatives (Parsons 1918; Cohen 1958; Thompson and Cornet 1981; Thompson 1984; Creel 1988; Connor 1989; Fenn 1989; Nichols 1989; Little 1998; Gundaker and McWillie 2005).

The potential ability of archaeologists to investigate the ways African cultural influences may have changed over time depend partly on the diversity of material they associate with an African influence. The reality is that archaeologists often seem unaware of the possible combination of African-derived cemetery landscape features. Archaeologists in recent decades have generally become aware that burials of African-descended people can include personal items on top of the grave, in the grave shaft, or in the coffin (Combes 1974; Jamieson 1995; Bruner 1996; Deetz 1996; Dockall, Powell, and Steele 1996; McCarthy 1997; Armstrong and Fleischman 2003; Davidson 2004; Fesler 2004; Smith 2008; Perry, Howson, and Bianca 2009; Smith 2010). However, for one of the slave burials at New Seville plantation in Jamaica, the archaeologists were not aware of the cultural significance of a large lock on top of a coffin until they saw the reactions of African-Jamaican site workers (Armstrong and Fleischman 2003, 46–47).

Some archaeologists have been reluctant to consider the cultural significance of other landscape components for people of African descent in the Americas. In the case of the African Burial Ground site, the original archaeological team was either unaware of or chose to ignore nonburial features that would have been components of an African-derived cemetery landscape (Perry, Howson, and Bianca 2009).

On Crooked Island, African-influenced cultural behaviors in cemeteries are still in practice in the early 2000s. The Crooked Island cemeteries, all of which were established between the mid-nineteenth through the early twentieth centuries, exhibit all of the culturally significant landscape features mentioned above, except for the faunal remains (Figure 2.1). Excavation of St. Matthew's Northern Burial Ground site provided an opportunity to investigate the historical existence of an African-derived cemetery cultural landscape and the ways this landscape was maintained or changed over time.

Figure 2.1. Gravesite of David Moss, Cripple Hill Cemetery, Crooked Island.

Personal Items Left on Graves

Personal objects left on top of graves are the most widely recognized aspect of an African-influenced cemetery landscape. This custom has been noted by cultural anthropologists, historians, and folklorists for sites in the United States and the Caribbean (Bolton 1891, 214; Parsons 1918, 88; Cohen 1958, 95; Georgia Writers' Project 1972, 54, 109; Jordan 1982, 21; Thompson 1984, 132–134; Creel 1988, 317; Connor 1989, 54; Fenn 1989, 45–46; Nichols 1989, 13–14, 18; Vlach 1991, 43–45; Nigh 1997, 168, 170; Little 1998, 248; Gundaker and McWillie 2005, 36).

In July 2002, I visited a number of cemeteries on Crooked Island, some of which belonged to settlements that are now abandoned. Crooked Island is located along the eastern edge of the Crooked Island Passage, the deepest channel that passes through the Bahamian archipelago. Documentary and archaeological evidence suggests that this location allowed the residents of Crooked Island considerable independence from the colony's administrative center in Nassau on New Providence Island, several hundred miles to the north (Turner 2006). In the late nineteenth and early twentieth centuries, the Bahamians who migrated to Panama to construct the trans-isthmus canal came from Crooked Island, Acklins, and nearby Fortune Cay. Until the start of World War I, German steamships en route to ports in South America routinely stopped at these islands to hire men for work as stevedores (Bahamas, Department of Archives 1986). Access to these wage-earning opportunities provided some Crooked Island residents better incomes than was available to African-Bahamians on most other islands in the colony at the time.

In researching for this book, I visited settlement cemeteries named Brown's, Thompson Hill, Moss Town, True Blue, Cripple Hill, and Colonel Hill. Except for the cemetery at Colonel Hill (the island's administrative center), these cemeteries were on dune ridges near the ocean. The most prominent feature in these cemetery spaces were the personal items left on top of each grave. These generally included a receptacle for food such as a plate or bowl, a drinking vessel, such as a tumbler, cup, or mug; and sometimes an eating utensil or other container such as a teapot (Figure 2.2). I have interpreted these as personal items that belonged to the individual. Sometimes these were favorite items, or they could have been the last eating containers the deceased individual used (Parsons 1918, 88). In the Bahamas, cultural behavior such as placing personal items on top of graves is part of a cultural landscape because this feature is not found in isolation from other African-derived cemetery landscape features.

Crooked Island is the only other island in the Bahamas where I documented evidence that this cultural behavior was practiced since at least the mid-nineteenth century and continued to the recent past (Figure 2.3). On other Bahama Islands, such as San Salvador, Eleuthera, and Exuma, the placement of a tree or plant at the head of graves is a noticeable landscape feature, as is the location of a cemetery near a body of water. A location near water is the most common landscape feature for any Bahamian cemetery that was established before the twentieth century. However, only on Crooked Island did the habit of leaving personal items on top of graves con-

Figure 2.2. Dishes on a grave in Thompson Hill Cemetery, Crooked Island.

tinue into the early twenty-first century. Other archaeologists have interpreted this cultural behavior as enhancing and maintaining an individual's social identity within a group (Perry and Paynter 1999; McCarthy 2006; Blouet 2014; Ogundiran and Saunders 2014).

In some Crooked Island cemeteries, a hole was made in the base of ceramic items before these were placed on a grave (Figure 2.4). This practice has been observed in the Congo region of West Africa and in African American cemeteries across the U.S. South (Glave 1891; Ingersoll 1892; Puckett 1926; Thompson 1984; Sobel 1988; Fenn 1989; Nichols 1989; Vlach 1990; Falola 2001). Some community residents explain that this action is intended to release the soul of the deceased person from the container, although it has been noted that in other cases residents had no explanation except that this is a long-standing tradition (Puckett 1926, 105; Georgia Writers' Project 1972; Sobel 1988, 198). In other Crooked Island cemeteries, items placed on graves were not altered. There was no evidence in any

Figure 2.3. Dishes atop nineteenth-century tombs, Thompson Hill Cemetery, Crooked Island.

Figure 2.4. Ceramic bowl with base removed, Crooked Island.

Crooked Island cemetery of the combination of these two practices—leaving complete ceramic vessels and leaving ceramic vessels with holes in the base. This difference in the disposition of ceramic vessels likely represents a variation in how different communities of African-Bahamians interpreted this cultural behavior. Elsie Parsons (1918, 88) referred to the tradition of placing personal "favored" items on a grave at Andros, but she did not note that these were first broken before being placed on the grave. These examples suggest that in the Bahamas (even in one island) there has historically been some variation in how this custom was observed.

Because African-Bahamians continue to believe in the spiritual power of cemeteries, locals stay away from them unless they are attending a funeral or are visiting the graves of relatives on special occasions. However, I became aware that some North American vacation residents who learned of grave items over a century old had gone on a rampage, collecting almost all of these articles except those that had been broken. Research photos I took in these cemeteries in 2002 are now the only surviving evidence of past cultural influences.

Trees and Plants as Memorial Grave Markers

There is a growing understanding among archaeologists of the use of trees by people of African heritage in association with burials (Lenik 2005; Blouet 2010; Rainville 2011; Delle and Fellows 2014). Documentary evidence indicates that some Africans, even in the Americas, referred to these trees as sacred groves where spirits and deities dwelled (Lenik 2005, 34; Brown 2002, 306–307). In West and Central Africa, sacred groves, whether they contain a single tree or group of trees, are locations that serve as historical markers for sites of initiation, burial, and other rituals (Chouin 2008, 179; Ross 2008; Sheridan 2008, 20). Because of their generally low status in the Americas, Africans were often unable to maintain many aspects of their native communal landscape. Yet even though they had to live in restricted circumstances, Africans in the Diaspora created landscapes that were culturally significant for them whenever possible. Examining the daily lives of Africans in the Americas (represented here by burial memorials) allows researchers to look at questions of continuity and change over time.

On Crooked Island, which plants or trees are used depends on the distance from the ocean and the level of salt in the environment. In cemeteries closest to the ocean, these plantings include native species of spider lilies (*Hymenocallis caribaea* and *H. latifolia*) and palms (*Leucothrinax morrisii*) (Broome, Sabir, and Carrington 2007). In cemeteries farthest from the sea or cemeteries that have an accessible source of fresh water, gum elemi (*Busera simaruba*) (Correll and Correll 1982) trees are used exclusively (Figure 2.5). In the Bahamas, cemeteries established in the nineteenth or early twentieth centuries were most often located in a few hundred yards of the water's edge. It seems that one reason why gum elemi was the preferred native tree species for grave monuments is because of the Bahamian folk belief that this tree thrives only where there is a source of fresh water. Gum elemi trees thus represented the presence of water regardless of whether a cemetery could be located near the ocean. Other reasons why the gum elemi would have been preferred are that it is a fast-growing tree and is one of the taller trees native to these islands.

When asked why a tree or plant was placed at the head of graves, Anafaye Knowles, a former teacher from Colonel Hill, Crooked Island, explained that the growth of the plant or tree is meant to symbolize the continued thriving of the deceased person's spirit even in death. In this way, these grave plantings serve as a living memorial to the deceased individual (see also Brown 2002). On the Family Islands, the preferred tree at graves is the gum elemi (Figure 2.6). In the two eighteenth-century black cemeteries in Nassau, gum elemi was used, as were large trees that have been introduced such as tamarind (*Tamarindus indica*) and woman's tongue (*Albizia lebbeck*) (Correll and Correll 1982).

Examples of these trees still stand at the head of a grave in the cemetery on the western edge of Nassau historically known as Bethlehem (Figure 2.7). Although Bethlehem still has some tree monuments that originally stood at the head of graves, there is now no evidence of personal grave goods. It should be noted, though, that this cemetery was made into a public park early in the twentieth century. While the trees, tombs, and stone grave markers were left in place, there is no way of knowing what this cemetery landscape looked like before it was repurposed.[1] There are no known images of this cemetery before it became a park.

Figure 2.5. Gum elemi grave memorials, Colonel Hill Cemetery, Crooked Island.

Figure 2.6. Gum elemi grave memorials, Cockburn Town Cemetery, San Salvador.

Figure 2.7. Grave memorial trees, Bethlehem Cemetery, Nassau.

The public cemetery for Cockburn Town, San Salvador, dates to the nine-teenth century and has several gum elemi grave monuments, but there is no evidence of any personal items left on graves. This cemetery is adjacent to the public road that encircles the island, so it is visible and easily acces-sible. One possibility is that nonlocal visitors to the island removed antique items from grave sites. Another is that any personal items left on graves were washed out to sea during heavy storm surges; the western edge of this cemetery is the beach at the southern edge of Cockburn Town's harbor. Yet another possibility is that no personal items were left on these graves.

Location near Water

One other feature I explored is the significance of a cemetery's location near a body of water. Cultural anthropologists and folklorists such as Cohen (1958), Creel (1988), Fenn (1989), Nichols (1989), and Gundaker and Mc-Willie (2005) who have examined black cemeteries and burial traditions in the Americas have noted the significance of bodies of water or representa-tions of water associated with burials and memorials for the dead. Histori-cal archaeologists have not noted this particular feature as a consideration for African-descended people when situating a cemetery, even though his-torically this has been a significant consideration for African-descended people in the Atlantic Diaspora. Enslaved laborers on plantations were more limited in the extent to which they were able to structure their own lives. This was less of an issue for free people of color and enslaved workers who were hired out to work in urban areas.

On islands in the Bahamas it is most common for community cemeter-ies to be located near the ocean. African-Bahamians emphasized this point in their conversations with me. The Bahamas are small, narrow islands, but it should not be assumed that locating a cemetery close to the ocean was historically the most feasible option on small islands with limited areas of deep soil. A primary consideration when situating a cemetery near the ocean would be finding a site that was protected from being inundated dur-ing a hurricane. The erosion created by high winds blowing grains of sand and salt spray against locally made or expensive imported grave markers over time is more difficult to protect against.

In the present, it is often assumed that areas blacks used for cemeter-ies were marginal lands of little use or value in the dominant society and that these were the only viable areas that African-descended people were allowed to use since they were always accorded the lowest social rank (Chicora Foundation 1996; Smith 2010, 41). Such an interpretation is unsatisfactory from the perspective of a historic African-descended population because it ignores the role of individual agency, particularly in the case of blacks living in urban environments. Communities of African-descended people appreciated the importance of maneuvering and negotiating within the racialized social order to attain significant community goals such as choosing where and how to bury and commemorate their dead. The community that used the Northern Burial Ground was able to establish a cemetery that suited their cultural preferences in a highly visible location at the eastern edge of the town. The next chapter will examine the historical development of European-based cemetery landscapes in order to emphasize the point that features that are generally found in those spaces are culturally distinct and can be identified archaeologically.

A number of cemeteries that were used by African-descended people and have been investigated archaeologically were originally located nearby a body of water. These include the African Burial Ground in New York (Perry, Howson, and Bianca 2009, 44); the Fontabelle and Pierhead cemeteries in Bridgetown, Barbados (Farmer, Smith, and Watson 2005, 678–679); the Utopia Quarter cemetery near Williamsburg, Virginia (Fesler 2004, 170); the Burial Ground for Negroes in Richmond, Virginia (Stevenson 2008, 2–3); Black Bottom Memorial Cemetery in Belhaven, North Carolina (Smith 2010, 38, 41); and Plantation Waterloo cemetery in Suriname (Watters 1994, 68) As these cemeteries have closed and urban areas have expanded, the pattern has been to cover over these early black cemeteries to facilitate new development (Farmer, Smith, and Watson 2005; Perry, Howson, and Bianca 2009; Stevenson 2008). The fact that such cemeteries had belonged to communities with little political or economic power meant the land was available to developers without regard for the concern of those communities. This kind of development history has heightened the cultural sensitivities of the broad descendant community when a historic cemetery is rediscovered decades or even centuries later.

Bahamians of African descent do not have any ready explanations for why cemeteries are so commonly situated near bodies of water. Sandra Greene (2002) and Wyatt MacGaffey (1986), writing about parts of West and Central Africa, noted the significance of bodies of water for com-memorating and honoring ancestral spirits. Researchers studying African American cemeteries in the U.S. South have recorded several rationales for the significance of burials near water. Explanations include providing a pathway between the worlds of the living and the spirit realm and the ability to travel back to Africa (Cohen 1958; Georgia Writers' Project 1972). Although the rationales for why burials are located near water vary, it is im-portant to note that for reasons of spiritual significance rather than simply as a practical matter, Africans in the Atlantic Diaspora preferred to situate their cemeteries near bodies of water.

Faunal Remains—Evidence of Feasting/Offerings

Archaeologists often investigate African Diaspora cemetery sites only after they have been impacted by later development or have been rediscovered in the course of new development. Because of this, it is difficult to make any association with isolated finds that seem to have been separated from the original cultural context. Without additional evidence to indicate that an artifact was intentionally used and deposited in the area where it is recov-ered, it is not possible to make any definitive cultural associations. (Watters 1994, 61–64). Although the original context of the Northern Burial Ground was disturbed by later developments such as sidewalk construction, I have assumed that any materials excavated from this site were not randomly deposited but became part of the site as a result of its earlier use as a cem-etery. Thus, a fourth landscape feature I considered is the evidence of faunal remains associated with cemeteries historically used by people of African descent. Cultural anthropologists and folklorists have noted the presence of animal bones, whether as food or sacrificial offerings; these have also been noted in historical documents (Parsons 1918, 88; Georgia Writers' Project 1972, 54, 106, 135, 140, 159, 182, 184; Vlach 1978, 144; McCarthy 1997, 372; Gundaker and McWillie 2005, 187).

This feature has not been noted in any extant Bahamian cemeteries. There are several possible explanations for this absence. Perhaps this cultural ac-tivity did not take place in a cemetery space. Perhaps cleaning and main-taining the cemetery space eliminated this feature. Elsie Parsons (1918) noted that on Andros Island a bowl of food was put out for the deceased in a corner of the yard. As with other African-derived mortuary behavior, the observance of food offerings or animal sacrifices not only varied among communities but also changed over time. It is possible that in some African-Bahamian communities, food offerings were usually left in the house yard of the deceased and that in other communities the practice was to leave food offerings in the cemetery at the gravesite.

The Case for African Cultural Connections

By the 1980s, scholars researching the African Diaspora in the Americas aimed to build on Herskovits's argument in the earlier debate on cultural retentions that despite the psychological ravages of slavery, African-descended people had retained elements of their African cultural heritage. The objective of these scholars was to identify African cultural retentions in the Americas and correlate them with specific ethnic groups in West Africa (Schuyler 1980; Thompson 1984; Vlach 1991). Archaeologists contributed to this debate by looking for evidence that socially defined racial groups treated similar objects differently (Fennell 2003; Ferguson 1992; Orser 1998; Heath and Bennett 2000; Wilkie 2000).

Africanist researchers critiqued this approach because it treated the extensive regions of West and Central Africa as static cultural zones with discreet culture areas for individual ethnic groups (Singleton 2001). It is now understood that ethnic groups in Africa historically developed cultural behaviors that were often similar to those of their neighbors (Thornton 1998). Variations of any particular cultural behavior is usually evident among a number of ethnic groups. This limited variation in expressions of symbols, beliefs, and ideas in material culture is what Africanist archaeologists refer to as a "symbolic reservoir" (Sterner 1992, 171–172). It is my interpretation that certain historic cemetery landscape features were derived from an African cultural heritage rather than from the dominant European cultural heritage, even though the artifacts themselves, such as the vessels discussed above, were usually of European origin. To support such a position, archaeologists must take into account not only the immediate context of use but also the historical and cultural position of the users.

Those who do research on West Africa make the point that ethnographic comparisons of Africans in the Americas with West and Central African people should consider the extent of European contact during the period being examined and the level of cultural exchange and interaction in a broad geographical region (Holl 2001; Kelly 2001; Maceachern 2001; Singleton 2001; Stahl 2001; Monroe and Ogundiran 2012). In West and Central Africa before European contact, where and how individuals were buried depended on who the person was and the manner of death. A number of ethnic groups buried relatives in the floor of the house in which they had lived. Among the Akan of Ghana, burial grounds before European contact were not marked in ways that Europeans would have recognized. Instead, the surrounding landscape was deliberately left in its natural and unaltered state (DeCorse 2001, 188). In his excavation of the town of Elmina, Christopher DeCorse focused on continuity and change as the critical issues for understanding the African perspective on contact with Europeans. DeCorse noted, "Because the funerary complex involves various artifacts and features, as well as the burial itself, it provides one of the best loci for the archaeological definition of *worldview*" (ibid., 187).

Douglas Armstrong and Mark Fleischman (2003) discovered four house-yard burials for enslaved workers at Seville plantation in Jamaica. They noted that no further yard burials could be located in the later-period slave village that was occupied from the 1780s to the 1890s (Armstrong and Fleischman 2003, 37–38). The authors remarked that eighteenth-century British writers noted only that enslaved workers buried loved ones in house floors or in the yard but were aware of the importance of allowing enslaved laborers to maintain connections that tied them even more closely to the land. These four burials were significant even in this earlier slave village (1670s–1780s), as they appear to be the only burials made in house yards. This suggests that these individuals had special status in this community (Armstrong and Fleischman 2003, 35, 40–42). Sandra Greene (2002) noted that in West and Central Africa, the Anlo-Ewe of Ghana historically buried relatives in the floor of the house where the deceased had lived. Similarly, Wyatt MacGaffey (1986, 55–56) reported that the BaKongo buried a chief and his attendants in his household compound.

Until the early nineteenth century, trees were not a major feature of western-style cemeteries (Rodwell 1989, 145–146). Yet the spiritual beliefs of many West and Central African groups involved the belief that certain trees could house ancestral spirits. Sandra Greene illustrates the historical impact of European colonial rule and Christian missionary work on the Anlo of Notsie in south-central Togo. Ethnic Anlo historically lived throughout southeastern Ghana and southern Togo. Anlo beliefs about the significance of water and trees in relation to burials are especially significant. As Greene states, "Nineteenth-century Anlos associated spiritual forces with the material reality of their built environment. . . . They believed that spiritual forces were capable of manifesting themselves not only in houses and in shrines, in streets and cemeteries but everywhere: in the air, in water bodies, in distant towns, in the earth, in the groves that dotted the Anlo landscape. Whether these places were encountered rarely or formed part of the quotidian rhythms of daily life, all were viewed as sites with multiple meanings, as both material objects and as containers of the sacred" (Greene 2002, 68).

Like the Anlo, many other ethnic groups in West and Central Africa ascribed spiritual significance to material elements of their natural and built environments (MacGaffey 1986; Greene 2002; Monroe and Ogundiran 2012). In the restricted life circumstances of the Diaspora in the Americas, African-descended people could most often express this connection between the realms of the physical and spiritual worlds in cemeteries. This entailed combining several landscape features such as burials, sacred groves, commemorative shrines, and associated activities such as sacrifices or ritual feasts into a single space. In West and Central Africa, these were all separate features in the cultural landscape (David 1992; Greene 2002; Sterner 1992; Vivian 1992).

Trees and plants that were used as burial monuments in the Bahamas can be understood as deriving from the widespread cultural use of sacred groves and sacred trees as repositories for ancestors and spirits in much of Africa and in Cuba, Haiti, the United States, and elsewhere in the Diaspora where similar uses have been found (Thompson 1984; Gundaker and McWillie 2002; Giles-Vernick 2002; Weiss 2003; Cabrera 2004; Sheridan and Nyamweru 2008). For example, in the U.S. Virgin Islands, spiritually significant tamarind trees were not always planted in a cemetery but were understood to be associated with a cemetery that was located nearby (Lenik 2005). As some archaeologists have noted, even in early plantation contexts, some planters allowed enslaved African workers to memorialize their dead however they chose (Armstrong and Fleischman 2003, 40–41). Some ethnohistorical accounts also suggest that Africans in the Diaspora were sometimes given cultural freedom in how they memorialized their dead (Orderson [1842] 2002, 43; Medford 2004, 175).

Archaeologists have rarely attempted to investigate the fourth African-derived cemetery landscape feature, evidence of feasting or animal sacrifice. Butchered faunal remains could be evidence of such cultural activity. In the Americas, there are references in the ethnohistorical literature to food offerings being left for the spirit of the deceased (Parsons 1918; Georgia Writers' Project 1972; Vlach 1978; McCarthy 1997; Gundaker and McWillie 2005). The failure of archaeologists to pay attention to these details may be related to the often-accidental means by which archaeologists become aware of unmarked cemetery sites. Even in the case of known cemeteries, archaeologists usually have not investigated sites with an understanding that there could be an array of deliberate landscape cultural features.

Archaeological evidence of ritual food offerings is most tenuous from sites in West and Central Africa. Environmental conditions such as high temperatures, rainfall, and acidic soils facilitate rapid deterioration of organic material, including bone (Kelly 2001, 92). Additionally, meat prepared for meals was generally cut into small pieces and any archaeological remains are tiny fragments (DeCorse 2001, 113; Kelly 2001, 92). Ethnohistorical information about *asensie* in sites in southern Ghana suggest that these were memorial sites where relatives left offerings of food and a ceramic representation of the deceased (Vivian 1992, 157–159). (*Asensie* are ceramic figurines that represent deceased relatives that were placed at the foot of trees where relatives believed they could commune with the spirit of the deceased.)

Evidence of funerary food offerings in the Americas is best understood in the context of continuity and change. Although African captives who were enslaved in the Americas belonged to many ethnic groups in West and Central Africa, there is ethnohistorical evidence that a number of these groups engaged in the practice of leaving funerary food offerings. However, ethnohistorical evidence suggests that this cultural practice was continued as an aspect of funerary observances in some African-descended communities in the Americas.

European Influence on Eighteenth- and Nineteenth-Century Cemeteries

To present the case for an African-influenced cemetery landscape, it is necessary to examine European-style cemetery spaces to make it clear how these spaces differ. Since the Bahamas remained a British colony for over 300 years, this chapter will examine the development of cemetery spaces in Great Britain and in colonial territories in the Americas.

In pre-Christian Britain, pagan burials commonly included a variety of grave goods. Pagan burial customs were gradually replaced by Christian burial rites. Although Christian burial customs generally did not involve grave goods, there have been instances where grave goods indicative of pagan beliefs were placed in graves in a Christian burial ground after the medieval period. In a burial ground at Barton-on-Humber, for example, grave goods dating to the period 1500–1750 that archaeologists have recovered included dice, several coins, a ceramic dinner plate, and a tin enamel-glazed sugar bowl (Rodwell 1989, 165).

Perhaps Richard Morris has provided the best archaeological description of the cultural progression from pagan to Christian cemeteries in Britain: "The picture which has been discerned in parts of west and north Britain is essentially that of a sequence. Chapels and churches are typically to be found as developments out of earlier cemeteries, which themselves were transformed from 'mere collections of inhumation graves' through increasingly formal stages. Pagan cemeteries could develop into Christian graveyards, and by addition of a church evolve into a parish churchyard" (Morris 1983, 51).

Beginning in the 1530s, the Reformation in England had a profound impact on land owned by Roman Catholic monasteries. As monasteries were dissolved, some of their property was granted to communities for use as churchyards and burial grounds (Rodwell 1989, 153–156; Gilchrist and Sloane 2005, 31–37; Willsher 2005, 11–12). During the Reformation, burials inside churches were outlawed. Although the practice continued for some time, this change meant that more burials were located in churchyards. However, churchyards were not set aside exclusively for burials. They were also the site of activities such as fairs and markets, children's playgrounds, arrow practice, the display of weapons for inspection, and a meeting place for trade associations (Gilchrist and Sloane 2005, 44–46; Willsher 2005, 11–14).

The burial spaces we know today as cemeteries were first being created by the second half of the eighteenth century. Cemetery spaces are defined by several characteristics that distinguish them from burial grounds, particularly those located in churchyards. Burial grounds were not established to serve a general populace; they served a smaller, limited group of people. The characteristics of cemeteries most relevant to this study include the following:

- Cemeteries generally serve an entire district or town; including people of any denomination (Rugg 2000, 270; Willsher 2005, 21).
- Cemeteries are usually located close to but not necessarily in a settlement or town (Rugg 2000, 261).

The landscaped, park-like spaces that are now so common as cemeteries date to the nineteenth century (Rugg 2000, 260; Willsher 2005, 21). Landscaping in these spaces often include large shade trees and pathways to enhance the peaceful, park-like atmosphere (Rugg 2000, 160; Willsher 2005, 21). Although deliberate landscaping of churchyards using trees began in the eighteenth century, trees, especially yews, had been planted in British church yards for hundreds of years before that time. After several centuries of continuous use and reorganization, it is generally no longer possible to determine whether these trees were originally planted as grave markers or as property markers (Rodwell 1989, 145–146).

By the second half of the eighteenth century, there was an understanding of possible health risks if dead bodies were interred too close to living populations, so regulations were established requiring cemeteries to be located on the outskirts of any settled area (Rugg 2000, 261).

In British West Indian colonies the Anglican Church was the state-recognized religious denomination. Stipends for Anglican clergy and construction costs for Anglican churches were approved by colonial assemblies.[1] As part of their responsibilities Anglican Church officials oversaw the administration and maintenance of all public cemeteries, such as the Northern Burial Ground in Nassau.

Interment in public cemeteries was not limited to black or white Anglicans. In the eighteenth century, five public cemeteries were established around Nassau. Centre Burial Ground and Northern Burial Ground (both of which I believe date to the first half of the eighteenth century) were located in the eastern part of the town, as was the Eastern Cemetery. Potter's Field,[2] which was originally for non-Anglican whites, and Bethlehem cemetery, which was for blacks, both of which were established around 1789,[3] were in the western part of Nassau.[4] By the early 1900s, Potter's Field was also known as the Western Cemetery.[5]

Since Britain had a cultural tradition that allowed public cemeteries to be used for functions apart from burials, it did not seem surprising that African people and their descendants in urban settings were generally allowed to use a public space to bury their dead as they saw fit. White colonists and officials did not object to African-descended communities maintaining separate cemetery spaces where they practiced African-derived burial customs to memorialize their dead. In *Creoleana*, his book about Bridgetown, Barbados, around the mid-1770s, J. W. Orderson described slave funerals he had observed at the Fontabelle slave cemetery on the western edge of the town. He wrote, "It was no unusual thing to see, as each Sunday returned, hundreds—nay, thousands of these poor deluded creatures 'throwing victuals,' and with drumming, dancing and riot practicing frenzied incantations over the graves of their deceased relatives and friends!" (Orderson [1842] 2002, 43). Even on some plantations this would have been the case. On the early Seville plantation in Jamaica, for example, the European masters and overseers did not create cemeteries that were rigidly controlled, park-like spaces. The concept of the landscaped cemetery did not develop until the late eighteenth century and did not become the standard until the nineteenth century (Rugg 2000, 261; Willsher 2005, 21). On plantations and in urban contexts, the establishment of separate burial areas for people of African and European descent also reflected the differential social statuses of these two groups.

The Archaeology of European-Style Cemetery Spaces in the Bahamas

New Providence was not the first island in the Bahamas English colonists settled in the mid-seventeenth century, but the capital, Nassau, is where the earliest architectural remains are located. This includes cemeteries. By the early eighteenth century there were at least two cemeteries in the town. The earliest cemetery was in the center of town near the Anglican church. The second cemetery was likely opened in the 1720s after the town's long and raucous period as a pirate haven had ended.

The British Crown took direct responsibility for governing the colony only after pirates had made the islands their headquarters and governing authority collapsed for about fifteen years. A new royal governor arrived in 1718 with the authority to offer pirates a full pardon if they voluntarily ended their illegal activity. This process took about ten years. An immediate result of having an effective system of government in place was the expansion of the tiny settlement on the island. The second cemetery, known from documentary records as Centre Burial Ground, was apparently part of this expansion. It was established on the eastern edge of the town. This location illustrates the view that developed in the eighteenth century that appropriate sites for cemeteries were best located away from the center of a town (Rugg 2000, 261).

Centre Burial Ground is now the earliest European-style cemetery in the Bahamas. The earlier mid-seventeenth century Christ Church cemetery in Nassau was destroyed in the early twentieth century and a building was constructed on the site. However, although the graves were presumably destroyed, the grave markers were removed and placed in the yard at Christ Church cathedral. Evidently there is a perception among the general populace (that still holds true today) that nothing remains of such old burials. There was no public resistance to the destruction of this seventeenth-century cemetery, likely because any descendants of the people buried there were either dead or no longer lived in the Bahamas. The early-twentieth-century community recognized no kinship with the cemetery population, so the decision to destroy the cemetery would have been seen as only a logistical matter of development planning.

I conducted emergency archaeological investigations in Centre Burial Ground in July and August 2002 because of the negative impacts on the site from a government agency's construction of a wall around it. To assess the extent of damage already done and in order to develop an appropriate management plan for this space, my aim was to uncover any partially visible grave sites, especially any that would be impacted by landscaping the site and constructing new paths. These excavations exposed grave sites that had been covered over by sand and crushed shell deposited by the storm surge from hurricanes in the late 1920s. The primary material excavated from the narrow spaces between graves was marble pebbles. Marble is neither indigenous to the Bahamas nor is it found in marine environments, so I interpreted these pebbles as landscaping material that at one time covered the spaces between graves. Another possible landscape feature exposed was the remains of walkways adjacent to grave sites in the southwest and northeast sections of the cemetery (Figure 3.1). These walkway remnants were constructed of bricks and interspersed with marble slabs. Both of these

Figure 3.1. Excavated grave sites, Centre Burial Ground, Nassau.

materials had to be imported, so these pieces represented expensive construction materials.

The other material remains that were excavated at this site all dated to the early twentieth century, likely the last time these surfaces were exposed. This would be consistent with the extensive flood damage caused by the 1926 and 1929 hurricanes. In the cleanup after this disaster, the northernmost segment of these burial grounds, the Northern Burial Ground across from Centre Burial Ground on East Bay Street, was not restored. The only cleanup in this central portion was concentrated on graves that remained fully above ground. The landscaping may have also included shade trees, but presently only one tree remains in the center of the site. At some time in the mid-twentieth century, circular concrete curbing that was put in around this tree damaged several graves.

The evidence of these fancy walkways along with the marble pebbles between grave sites suggests that this cemetery was expensively landscaped during at least part of the nineteenth century. The nineteenth century landscape in this cemetery would have created a serene, park-like atmosphere for visitors to this space. Such evidence situates this cemetery in the movement to create a park-like atmosphere in European-style cemeteries.

Although trees were used in both African Diaspora cemetery landscapes and in European-style cemeteries, beginning in the late eighteenth century, the cultural significance of these trees differed. In European-style cemeteries, landscape trees were planted to create shade and a tranquil atmosphere. Trees were also planted in park-style cemeteries in places that complemented the winding paths and curving lawns in the space. In urban cemeteries, it was especially important to integrate trees into the overall design in order to create a serene atmosphere for visitors to the space. In contrast, in African-derived cemetery landscapes, certain trees served as living memorials to ancestor spirits. Throughout the Diaspora, trees were often planted at the head of a grave, directly behind some other form of grave marker. These were often made of wood and were subject to deterioration, leaving the tree and the mounds or depressions in the ground surface as the main indications of a grave. In the Bahamas, the usual practice was to plant a memorial tree or plant at the head of each grave. These trees and plants, especially symbolic spider lilies, and other culturally significant landscape features created very different visual profiles in African-influenced cemetery spaces than the landscape of European-style cemeteries and their garden-like layout. In Governor's Harbour on Eleuthera, the residents still refer to the town's two cemeteries in racial terms. The "White Cemetery" overlooks the bay on the north coast, while the "Coloured Cemetery" is a few hundred meters away, overlooking the shallow southern coast. In the "White Cemetery," most graves are marked by headstones, many of which are made of imported marble, and there are no trees. In contrast, there are few headstones in the "Coloured Cemetery"; instead, there are a number of coconut trees and spider lilies scattered throughout the cemetery. These plantings were originally planted at the head of a grave, but except for the surviving plants, these graves are no longer visible on the current ground surface.

4

St. Matthew's Northern Burial Ground

Documents that reveal the history of St. Matthew's Northern Burial Ground were rediscovered in the 1990s by Irwin McSweeney, a former Anglican priest who was conducting archival research in the Jamaica National Archives in Spanish Town. Information on a Bahamian cemetery was archived in Jamaica because the cemetery could not be officially consecrated until 1826 by the newly appointed Bishop of Jamaica, the Right Rev. Christopher Lipscombe. The Bahamas were included in the Anglican Diocese of Jamaica, which was not created until 1824. The Anglican Church was the state church of Great Britain and was the denomination charged with establishing and maintaining the religious status of all British colonies.

After the arrival of Loyalist refugees in the Bahamas, St. Matthew's Parish was created in the 1790s on the eastern side of Nassau to accommodate the increased population (Bahamas, Public Records Office 1975, 19). Several new cemeteries were opened or expanded on the east and west sides of the town, but these spaces were not consecrated until some thirty years later, after the Diocese of Jamaica had been created and the new bishop could attend to these official duties. The record of this event stated:

An Act of Consecration and Dedication of three certain Lots or pieces of Ground as and for Cemeteries or Burial Grounds for the Interment of Persons dying Inhabitants of or within the Parish of Saint Matthew on the Island of New Providence, one of the Bahama Islands within the Diocese of Jamaica. On Saturday the twentieth day of May in the year of our Lord One Thousand eight hundred and twenty six The Right Reverend Father in God Christopher by divine permission Lord Bishop of Jamaica being invested with Episcopal robes and accompanied by The Reverend William Patterson.[1]

When he arrived at the church, the bishop was presented with a petition signed by the officiating minister of St. Matthew's church, the church wardens, and several local magistrates. This petition formally asked the bishop to consecrate three cemeteries administered by St. Matthew's church. Two of these cemeteries were set aside especially for white people. One was the area around the church that was bounded on the south by Shirley Street and by Dowdeswell Street to the north. The other cemetery, also known as Centre Burial Ground, predated the establishment of St. Matthew's Parish in 1796. This cemetery was likely established as early as the 1720s after the first royal governor, Woodes Rogers, successfully ended the turbulent years when the Bahamas, New Providence in particular, was a haven for pirates. The earliest surviving grave marker in Centre Burial Ground commemorated the life of Thomas Pinckney, who died in 1733 (Department of Archives, Nassau 1976, 52). This is now the oldest existing cemetery in the Bahamas. The third cemetery section the Bishop of Jamaica dedicated was set aside for the burial of blacks within the parish, both enslaved and free (Figure 4.1). After 1833, this cemetery was known simply as the Northern Burial Ground. The petitioners in 1826 explained that

> the Burial Grounds of the said Parish have been appropriated for the purpose of Interment for upwards of twenty years, and that the same were purchased several years ago. . . . That the Burial Ground of the said Parish appropriated for Black Persons and Persons of Colour fronts the Harbour of Nassau on the North and extending thereon Three Hundred and eighty feet, East on the Public Causeway or Road leading Eastwardly and extending thereon thirty nine feet, South on Bay Street and extending thereon Three Hundred and ninety feet, and bounded on the West by a Lot now possessed by a certain Mr Pye and extending thereon One Hundred and thirty five feet, which said several Burial Grounds have been properly enclosed and fenced in, and are now in all respects fit and ready for Consecration. Parish of St Matthew 16th May 1826.[2]

This document conveys the impression that all three of these cemetery sections were established at the same time in the late eighteenth century. However, the earliest legible dates on headstones in Centre Burial Ground indicate that this cemetery dates to the early eighteenth century. It is likely not coincidental that the cemetery for people of African descent was situated across the

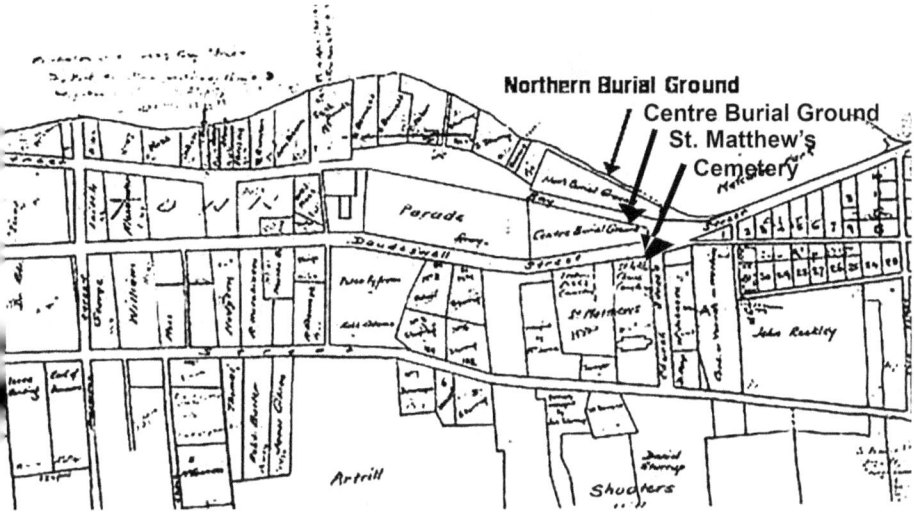

Figure 4.1. Plan showing the location of three burial grounds, 1826. Courtesy of Jamaica National Archives, Spanish Town, Jamaica.

street from Centre Burial Ground. After the Loyalist migration necessitated the creation of St. Matthew's Parish in 1796, construction of a church building began in 1800. The church was completed in 1802. It was likely during this period that land immediately surrounding the church building was used to establish a new cemetery. Therefore, it seems that St Matthew's Church Cemetery is the only one of the three cemetery sections associated with St Matthew's Church that was established at the end of the eighteenth century.

Before Loyalists migrated to the colony, there was no legislative policy to establish racially segregated public spaces such as cemeteries. Surviving eighteenth-century Christ Church registers for recording baptisms and marriages did not maintain separate listings for whites and non-whites until about 1790.[3] By this time Loyalist immigrants had apparently become members of the vestry, the church's governing body. Before 1790, nonwhites were noted by their color (i.e., black or mulatto) and their legal status (slave or free). The earliest surviving burial registers date to the early 1800s, by which time records for whites and "coloured" were routinely written in separate sections of the same register. The records for whites were written from the front of the book and the records for nonwhites were written at the back of the book, often with the top of the page reversed so that the "top" of the back pages was actually at the lower end of the book.[4]

The existence of a separate cemetery for people of color would suggest that such a cemetery was established by members of this community to meet their cultural needs. As noted in chapter 3, until the late eighteenth century, European-style cemeteries served a number of different uses. In urban areas in particular, African-descended people were generally free to create their own culturally distinct cemetery spaces (Delle and Fellows 2014, 481). It seems to have been the case that as long as a cemetery was not located on land that dominant social groups regarded as economically valuable, they had no complaint about these culturally distinct spaces. For the community of African-descended people, the high visibility of an African-influenced cemetery landscape was a public declaration of their cultural affiliation.

John McCarthy's findings from cemeteries used by Philadelphia's First African Baptist Church in the first half of the nineteenth century illustrate the point that people of African descent publicly displayed their cultural affiliation in their cemetery spaces. There was a significant difference in the amount of African-derived cultural materials associated with burials in two cemeteries this free black congregation used. In the earlier cemetery, which was in use from 1810 to 1822, only 2.4 to 5.9 percent of the 85 burials excavated contained cultural materials that could be interpreted as African-influenced burial practices. But McCarthy calculated that in the second cemetery, which was in use from 1824 to 1841, 11.4 percent of the 140 burials excavated contained cultural materials interpreted as African-influenced burial practices. McCarthy (1997, 378) considered that within the context of a highly racialized society, "the maintenance, or revival, of African-influenced burial customs at the 8th Street First African Baptist Church congregation fits into an overall pattern of in-migration, economic stress, and growing racism as a reactive expression of the community's vitality and resistance to domination. In this small way, the members of this congregation acted to define their community and shape their everyday sociocultural reality."

One indication of the way this free black Philadelphia community reinforced their community identity was their decision to revive aspects of their African cultural heritage, including burial customs. I argue that a similar dynamic was at work in Nassau, where St. Matthew's Northern Burial Ground shows a deliberate cultural shift at a particular time period. By the mid-nineteenth century, members of this community had decided that very public displays of African heritage were not to their social advantage. They seem to have decided that they could not fully engage with the wider society if they maintained a visible African cultural identity.

Based on the creation of similar African-derived cemetery practices in the African Burial Ground in New York and the First African Baptist Church cemetery in Philadelphia, it appears that African Diaspora communities in the Americas used such practices as leaving personal items inside or on top of graves, putting out food offerings, and planting memorial plants at the head of graves to signify membership within a community which opted to publicly display aspects of this African-derived cultural heritage. Decisions about whether to continue these practices seem to reflect how members of these communities viewed themselves in relation to the wider society. The free black community in Philadelphia chose to revive African-derived cemetery practices in the 1820s and 1830s. McCarthy interpreted this cultural change as a means of defining and reinforcing the African American community of Philadelphia, which lived in a hostile, increasingly racialized environment.

In contrast, the community that used the Northern Burial Ground continued African-derived cemetery practices for more than 100 years before discontinuing them. Although this Nassau community also lived in a racialized society, they seem to have decided to change their cultural behavior in the mid-nineteenth century in order to participate in new ways in the larger society. The cemetery treatment on Crooked Island, Bahamas, illustrates yet another way that African-descended people in the Americas choose to convey their cultural identity. Even in the early twenty-first century, some communities on this island were still leaving personal dishes on graves and planting trees at the head of a grave. If the presumption is that these cultural practices reflect cultural identity, then it appears that these Crooked Island communities have not been influenced to change their cultural identity to accommodate a larger society but instead have been able to engage with the wider world on their own terms.

Preservation History of the Site

Since the Northern Burial Ground was a public cemetery, the Board of Public Works maintained the perimeters of the site. The vestry of St. Matthew's Church paid to maintain the cemetery itself. By the mid-nineteenth century, the site was bounded on three sides by a two-foot-high stone wall topped by a wooden picket fence. Centre Burial Ground across the street had no wall. Could it be that this wall and wooden picket fence was intended to keep some things from public view? A sea wall was built along the waterfront in 1883. It was deemed necessary because the cemetery was at sea level and was prone to being inundated by storm surges during hurricanes. The height of the sea wall was raised again in the 1880s, and the wall was repaired around 1901.[5]

The last entry in St. Matthew's vestry minutes that recorded a cleaning of the Northern Burial Ground was in 1903, so it is likely that the cemetery was not used after this time.[6] When a sidewalk was constructed through the length of the cemetery in the 1930s, most of the skeletal remains and other cultural materials were gathered up and likely discarded. There is no record of outcry from the black community about this desecration, likely because the composition of that community had changed significantly. From the 1870s, there was a steady flow of outmigration from the Bahamas by those who sought wage-earning opportunities elsewhere in the region. The community that had historically used this cemetery would have certainly been affected by this outmigration.

Meanwhile, there was also considerable internal migration from other islands in the archipelago to Nassau, the colony's only urban area at the time.[7] Local boats coming to Nassau from the islands south of New Providence would have docked at Potter's Cay only about a quarter of a mile east of Northern Burial Ground. Many of these migrants, the majority of whom would also have been of African descent, would have settled in the communities near the dock. These would have been the communities that had historically used the Northern Burial Ground. By the 1930s, when the government chose to repurpose this cemetery site, the nearby black communities that had built and used this cemetery had already gone through a major population shift.

The only connection the new migrants to Nassau had to the Northern Burial Ground was the knowledge that it was a cemetery. In the community today, people are aware that this site was a cemetery but are generally unclear about where the cemetery was located. Most people assume that the cemetery site is the area currently on the waterfront. I had already commissioned a ground-penetrating radar (GPR) survey of the site before an elderly former resident of the area remembered that the sea wall she

Figure 4.2. Aerial photo showing the Northern Burial Ground site. Courtesy of the Department of Lands & Surveys, Nassau, Bahamas.

played on as a child was not the same one that is currently on the waterfront. This led me to examine aerial photographs of New Providence taken in the 1940s and 1950s (Figure 4.2). These images clearly showed that the land presently on the waterfront from this site was reclaimed sometime in the early 1960s. Fortunately, the GPR survey extended onto the grass verge between the reclaimed land and the street. This verge is actually the Northern Burial Ground site. Its nineteenth century sea wall is now at ground level and serves as the boundary between this historic cemetery site and the land that was reclaimed in the early 1960s.

Site Survey

I conducted a geophysical investigation of an area that was approximately 240 feet north to south by 290 feet east to west. The site is located north of

East Bay Street and west of the new Paradise Island bridge (GeoView 2007, 1–3). The purpose of the investigation was to help identify the existence and the location of any unmarked gravesites within the areas of investigation.

The GPR survey was conducted within the accessible portions of the site along a series of parallel transects spaced one to two feet apart. The GPR data was collected with a GSSI radar system using a 400-megahertz antenna with a time-range setting of 45 nanoseconds. This time-range setting provided information to an estimated depth of six to eight feet below land surface. A total of 236 GPR transects (radargrams) were collected at the site. The total linear footage of GPR data collected was 31,413 feet. The two-dimensional radargrams were then analyzed using GPR Slice to create three-dimensional time depth slices of the site.

The features observed on GPR data most commonly associated with graves are:

- An area of increase in the amplitude or laterally limited change of the GPR signal response at the particular depth intervals of interest. These changes in signal response can be the result of reflections from the target (i.e., gravesite) or from reflections from the altered soil horizons associated with the grave site.
- The occurrence of parabolic-shaped GPR reflectors within a laterally limited area. Depth of such GPR reflectors typically range from three to six feet below land surface. A parabolic GPR signal response is typically associated with a buried object. In the case of graves, the parabolic-shaped reflectors are usually created when the GPR antenna is pulled perpendicular to the long axis of a grave.
- In cases where gravesite remains have deteriorated, grave shafts can sometimes be determined by the presence of discontinuities in otherwise continuous soil horizons (represented by near-horizontal GPR reflectors). It is necessary to perform multiple closely spaced GPR transects across the suspect areas when characterizing such anomalies. When an area with discontinuous soil horizons has a rectilinear shape, it is possible that a grave is present at that location.

The probability that a GPR anomaly is associated with a grave increases as the number of previously discussed attributes are observed on the radargrams. It is not possible, based on the GPR data alone, to determine if a GPR anomaly is associated with a grave.

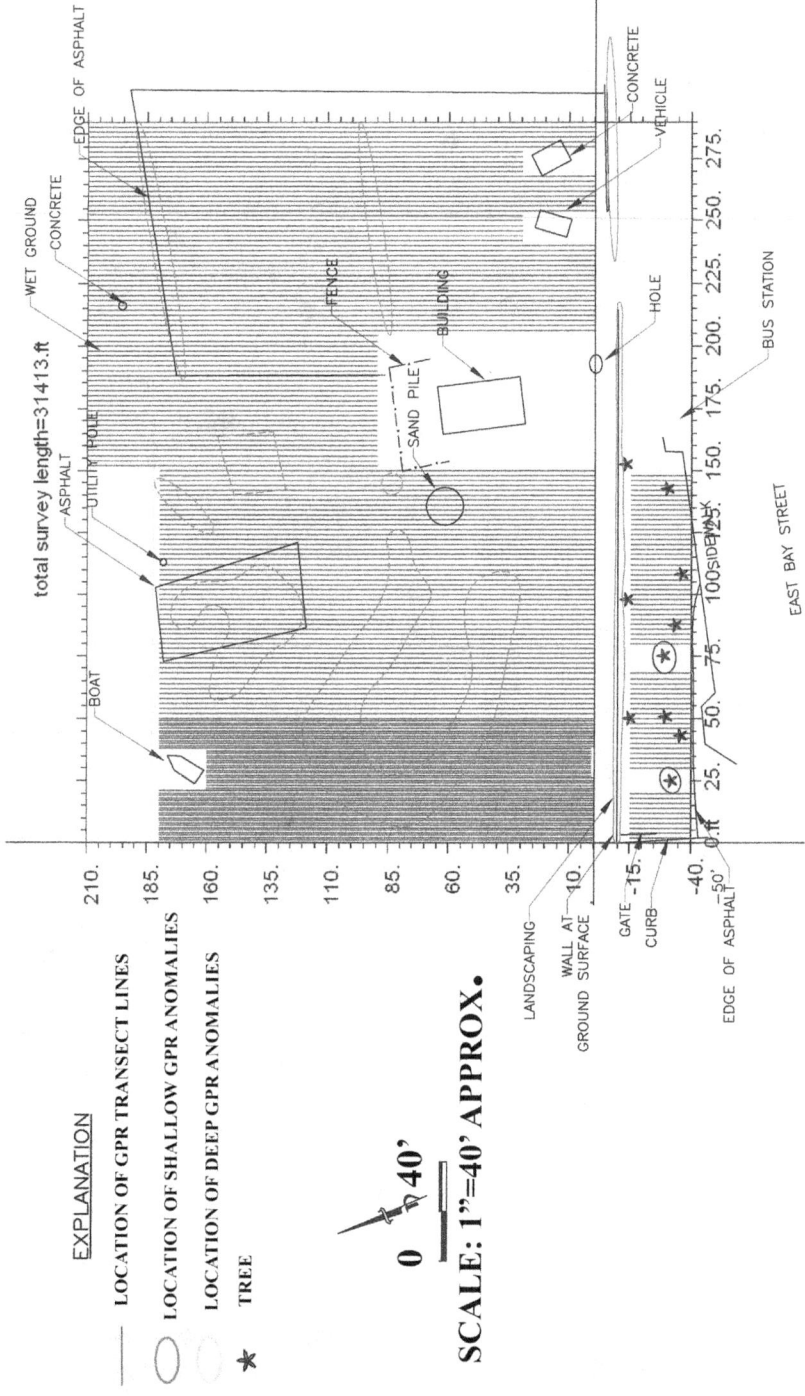

Figure 4.3. Site map showing the geophysical survey area of the Northern Burial Ground. The National Museum of the Bahamas, Antiquities, Monuments and Museum Corporation.

Survey Results

Nine GPR slices were created for the site at depths of 0–1 foot, 1–2 feet, and at 3, 4, 5, 6, 7, and 8 feet below land surface. Multiple anomalous areas were identified within the survey space. These GPR anomalies are divided into near-surface anomalies and deep anomalies.

Near-Surface Anomalies

The near-surface anomalies are visible from 0 to 3 feet below land surface. They are characterized by fairly large areas of subtle changes in the GPR signal response. This type of anomaly may be the result of changes in near-surface soils or may indicate foundations of structures or roadways that are now buried. These anomalies are most likely not associated with graves.

Deep Anomalies

Deep anomalies are evident from 4 to 8 feet below land surface. They are characterized by abrupt increases in the GPR signal response within a laterally limited area. It is more probable that deep anomalies are associated with gravesites. Numerous areas of elevated GPR signal responses were evident on the deeper GPR time slices. However, only deep anomalies that had the strongest GPR signal responses and were large enough to be associated with an adult grave were identified on the survey site maps.

Preliminary Excavations

Although mid-twentieth-century aerial photographs immediately clarified where the Northern Burial Ground was located, the GPR survey was extremely useful in helping determine a feasible spot to begin excavating. The survey identified an anomaly on the grass verge that was consistently associated with an elevated GPR signal down to eight feet below the surface, the lowest level tested. In the summer of 2008, test excavations were conducted at this site because a government agency was planning to situate a truck weigh station on the reclaimed land near the base of the bridge to Paradise Island.

The concern about these development plans was that when an exit for the truck weigh station was created, the remains of the Northern Burial Ground site would be negatively impacted yet again. The agency had refused to revise their plans because as they understood it, there were no extant remnants of

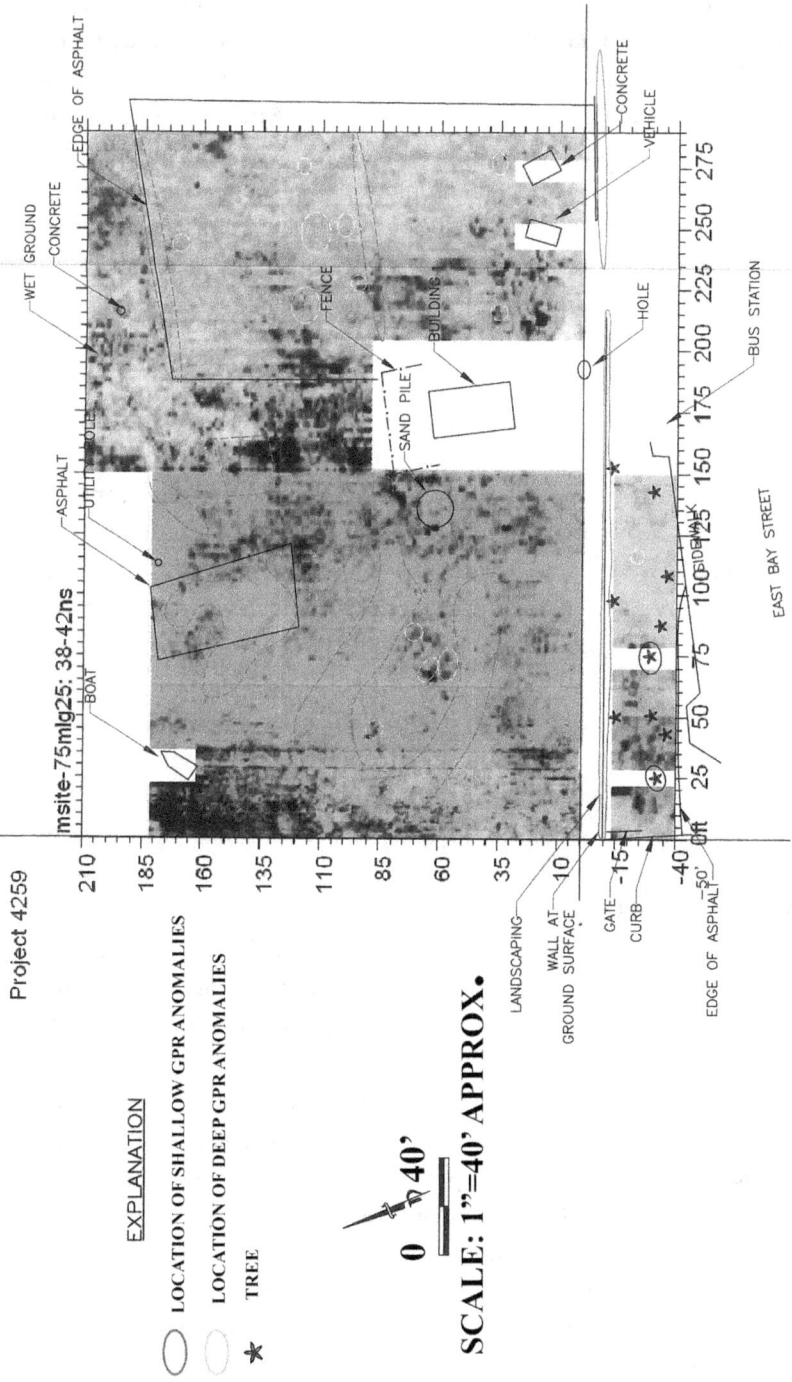

Figure 4.4. A deep anomaly on the geophysical survey time slice at eight feet below the surface. The National Museum of the Bahamas, Antiquities, Monuments and Museum Corporation.

the cemetery. The objective in conducting a test excavation was to recover definitive evidence that human remains were still buried within the site. The anomaly identified in the GPR survey corresponded with a surface depression on the ground. It is common in unmarked cemetery sites for some graves to be identified by a slight depression on the ground surface. With this in mind, a two-meter-square test unit was mapped out over this area.

For the preliminary excavations, there was a tight timeline of two to three weeks to excavate, process the findings, and submit a report in the hope of halting the proposed development plans. The crew had no archaeological field experience, so as much as possible I tried to assess what was being uncovered. This was an archaeological salvage operation, so the focus was on the materials that would be most helpful for assessing the history of this site. Because there was limited storage space in the archaeological lab facility at the National Museum of the Bahamas, I collected only a representative sample of large, heavy artifacts such as brick and shaped limestone. In the Bahamas, bricks were historically imported, usually entering the colony as ballast on ships. As a nonlocal product, bricks would have been a relatively expensive material. In a cemetery, bricks could have been used to construct above-ground tombs and curbing around gravesites. We did not collect brick at this site because although it is likely that it was originally associated with individual graves, it was out of context by now and I could only note that some grave sites had likely incorporated brick. The plan was also to document, but not to collect, the remains of headstones made of both imported and local materials unless there were extenuating circumstances. Because the site had been a public thoroughfare at least since a sidewalk was put in about eighty years ago, I initially anticipated that human skeletal remains would be the only bones collected; I planned to only note the presence of other bones. Twentieth-century materials were deposited at the site after it was no longer used as a cemetery. Among the artifacts that I interpreted as twentieth-century materials was evidence of food remains—the bones of chicken, fish, and machine-cut pork chops. Current dating techniques did not help in assessing a specific time period when these ecofacts were deposited, so my initial decision was to not collect these food remains and to note their presence within the site. However, this decision had to be revised when the team recovered butchered animal bones that had not been cut by machine. Evidence of non-machine butchering marks suggested that this meat had been butchered during an earlier period.

The excavation proceeded with arbitrary levels 20 centimeters deep. The unit was divided into one-meter quadrants to provide another measure of control in recording the context of any finds. As the site was originally at the water's edge, it was not surprising that water was seeping to the surface at about 60 centimeters. Because we had no pumping equipment to remove the water, only the southeast quadrant was excavated below level 2 (20 to 40 centimeters). The water was removed manually to allow time—less than three minutes—to assess the cultural material being exposed. This quadrant was selected for further investigation because the shaft of a femur was recovered from the damp sandy matrix at level 2.

Two wooden slats stacked vertically were exposed in this quadrant. They went no lower than a depth of 86 centimeters. Other finds associated with this wood included a number of metatarsals and phalanges (bones of the foot). This feature has been interpreted as the remains of a coffin, possibly made of pine. It seems that this part of one burial remained in situ even after the sidewalk was constructed.

Figure 4.5. Wood slats interpreted as the in situ remains of a coffin.

It appears that the segments of wooden slats are in the position in which they were originally placed. If these wood fragments are the remains of a burial, this suggests that burials within this cemetery were extremely shallow, as these remains are less than one meter below the current ground surface. Additionally, as this site was originally on the water's edge, I have assumed that burials within this site would have been placed in water. This was apparently a desirable practice for people of African descent. Elaine Nichols photographed several 1960s African American burials in which the coffin was lowered into a grave shaft with several inches of standing water (1989, 35). As early as 1804, the Bahamian Parliament passed legislation requiring grave shafts to be no less than four feet deep.[8] Is it possible that establishing this legal standard could have been prompted by the cultural behavior of Bahamians of African descent in preferring to make burials close to the waterfront?

The test unit produced an array of cultural materials that were quite enlightening about what could be expected about the condition of burial remains throughout the rest of the site. These included an almost complete white salt-glazed stoneware rimmed plate with a barleycorn rim design and the base of a mid- to late-eighteenth-century wine bottle. The most surprising finds, though, were the fragments of butchered faunal remains. Because the original archaeological context at this site was no longer intact, it was not possible to readily determine which faunal remains were deposited after the cemetery was closed. We did not collect chicken, porkchop, and fish bones that are still common today. The faunal bones the team recovered all showed some evidence of butchering using a hand saw or a machete. Meat butchered by these nonmechanical methods likely predates the close of this cemetery in the early 1900s.

Ceramics, shell, and stone fragments associated with a Lucayan site constituted another category of unanticipated finds. These would have predated any historic-era settlement of this island. Lucayan sites throughout the Bahamian archipelago are most often situated behind coastal dunes or the remnants of dunes. As more archaeological research is conducted on settlements of the later historic period, these kinds of layered sites will become more common. The Lucayan site was named Sheltered Harbour and recorded as SH 251.

The findings of the test indicated that significant evidence of human burials and associated grave treatments were still present within the site.

Because of these findings, plans for the proposed truck weigh station were relocated to another site in a less archaeologically sensitive area east of the bridge. I constructed a plan for more extensive investigations at this site. The goal was to understand whether a pattern of artifacts was consistent throughout the site. This would be helpful in developing a history of the site's use.

Site Excavations

A total of five units were excavated along the length of the site on both sides of the sidewalk. A government agency authorized the drilling of a row of holes about 18 inches in diameter from the western edge of the site to the bus-stop pavilion near the center of the site. Artifacts were collected from the soil exposed by the drilling of these holes. Unit 1 was positioned between two of the drill holes, at 17.7 meters east along the baseline on the sea wall and 9.3 meters south of the wall. Artifact finds from level 1 of this unit included small fragments of human bone, butchered beef bones, and ceramics dating from the eighteenth to the twentieth centuries. Also found were two mid-twentieth-century coins: a half-penny dating to the British colonial era that was locally known as a copper (the Bahamas transitioned from pounds sterling to dollars in 1966), and a U.S. penny. Unfortunately, the surfaces of both coins were too corroded to enable me to identify when they were minted. In level 2, a cutlery handle, possibly that of a spoon, was found. Two upright flat stones were uncovered in the southeast quadrant. The entire eastern half of this unit was taken down to a third level (40 to 60 centimeters) to understand what these stones could be. By 50 centimeters, water was seeping to the surface.

The two stones were unmarked and undecorated grave footstones carved from local limestone. No measurements were recorded for the full vertical height of these stones as they were still in place when they were uncovered. Only the dimensions for the top portions of these stones are noted here, as the plan was not to remove these stones from their original positions. The smaller of the two stones measures 21 centimeters wide. Its depth is 6 centimeters, and it has a domed top. The larger stone is rectangular and measures 27.5 centimeters across. Its depth is 5.5 centimeters (Figure 4.7). The bases were buried at about 89 centimeters below the surface. The stones were not removed but were photographed and re-buried. Removing the stones would

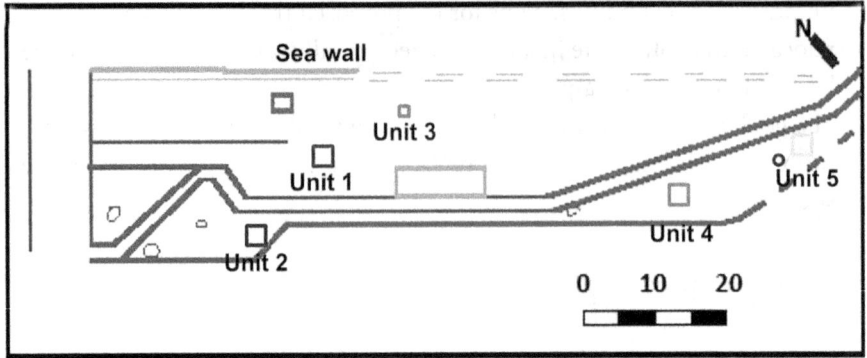

Figure 4.6. Excavation site map for Northern Burial Ground.

Figure 4.7. Two limestone footstones still in their original position.

have entailed devising an appropriate conservation plan to dehydrate and desalinate the stones, and this was beyond the scope of the project.

Unit 2 was situated 22 meters east along the baseline and 16.58 meters south of it. This unit was between the sidewalk and the street in the shade of a tree that will eventually be investigated as a likely descendant of a grave memorial tree. From level 1 (0 to 20 centimeters) a wide variety of eighteenth-, nineteenth-, and twentieth-century material remains were recovered. In level 2 (20 to 40 centimeters) of this unit, the crew recovered the largest cache of identifiable human skeletal remains from the site. These remains consisted of a cranial cap, the right half of the mandible, one clavicle, and some ribs and vertebrae (Figure 4.8). The profile of the unit's north wall where these remains were uncovered shows that the cranial cap was less than 10 centimeters below the base of the earliest sidewalk. This detail suggested that this cache of human remains had been gathered for removal and disposal off site. Evidently this cache of skeletal remains was not removed but instead was re-buried just below the sidewalk that was being constructed.

Figure 4.8. Human cranial cap in the wall of excavation Unit 2.

Figure 4.9. The first excavation team with the big find of the day; a human skull, ribs, and vertebrae.

A filigree gold brooch measuring 2.25 centimeters by 3 millimeters was recovered from the sandy matrix immediately beneath the cranium. Based on the likely association of this piece of clothing adornment with the remains nearby, it is likely that this individual was an adult female. The cranial features that are usually referenced in bioarchaeology for sex estimation, such as the supraorbital ridges and the chin, are missing or incomplete on this individual. Other cranial fragments were recovered from the southeast quadrant. I interpreted these remains as another individual because the bone of these cranial fragments was significantly thicker than the more complete cranium.

The next unit was located at the center of the site at 43 meters east along the baseline and 3 meters south of the baseline. Only one square meter of this unit was excavated. At a depth of just 7 centimeters there was bedrock; no artifacts were recovered from here. The topography of this unit suggests that at least a portion of this central area was unusable for burials.

The area immediately south of this unit is the bus-stop pavilion on the site. It was constructed atop a concrete foundation and opens onto the latest iteration of the sidewalk. Immediately south of the sidewalk, the exit from the street to the bridge was widened to allow vehicles to move out of the flow of traffic entering the bridge in order to pick up or drop off passengers at this bus stop. This configuration of new construction means that any remnant of the historic cemetery in this area has likely been destroyed.

The northern edge of the foundation of the bus-stop pavilion served as the baseline for Unit 4 because the nineteenth-century sea wall now extends only some 35 meters along the northern edge of the site. The pavilion's foundation is 5.23 meters long and is parallel to the line of the sea wall. Unit 4 was situated 16 meters east of the pavilion and two meters south of it. As noted for Unit 2, the sidewall profiles for this unit present evidence of an earlier sidewalk. Much of the concrete and asphalt was removed, but a layer of white marl is still visible on top of a layer of gray ash, or burned material. The soil layer immediately below this is extremely compacted, suggesting that this area may have been a well-trodden pathway before sidewalks were constructed across this site.

Artifacts from this unit included remains of large iron spikes that would be more consistent with an access area for small boats than with a quiet cemetery landscape. Aerial photographs from the 1940s and 1950s clearly show that by the mid-twentieth century the waterfront near the Northern Burial Ground site was an anchorage for small local vessels. Some of these boats were abandoned and were deteriorating at that time. This would explain the number of buried anomalies the GPR survey identified within the area of reclaimed land.

Skeletal remains recovered from this unit were fragmented; the damp, compacted sand presented a major challenge in attempts to remove already-fragile bones. Other artifactual remains were predominantly eighteenth-century ceramics and bottle glass. Excavation continued through two levels to end at 40 centimeters. No additional artifacts were being discovered and the color of the sand had changed from a pale brown color to a very light-colored sand. Both of these indicators suggested that this depth was near the lowest level of earliest historic-period use of the site.

The fifth and final unit excavated was situated at 46.5 meters east of the foundation of the bus-stop pavilion. This unit was near the narrow eastern edge of the site. The unit was about one meter east of a woman's tongue tree (*Albizia lebbeck*) that was possibly planted as part of an African-influenced cemetery landscape. As with Unit 4, the majority of artifacts recovered from this unit date to the eighteenth and early nineteenth centuries. We also recovered mid-twentieth-century artifacts that would have certainly been deposited at this site well after the cemetery was closed in the early 1900s and had been covered over by hurricane storm surge in the 1920s. A chunk of stone that surfaced in level 2 (20–40 centimeters) was originally thought to be a fragment of concrete from an earlier sidewalk. Excavation into level 3 (40–60 centimeters) revealed that this was actually part of a headstone carved from local limestone. This headstone appears to have been pushed face down and covered over by the base of the earliest sidewalk.

Figure 4.10. Limestone headstone buried below the ca. 1930s sidewalk.

Lab Processing

As this is a waterlogged site that was originally on the harbor front, it was important that all of the excavated materials except ferrous metals be desalinated and dehydrated in the lab before being cataloged and stored. Excavated finds from each level were first sorted by material in the lab, then soaked in fresh water for at least three days. The most affordable and available dehydrating agent was 70 percent isopropyl alcohol. After being soaked in water, smaller sherds and artifacts were put in alcohol for another three to four days. Materials that were thicker, heavier, and denser, such as brick and limestone, were soaked at each phase for at least one week. Once materials had been through both soaking phases, they were spread out to dry for at least one week. Next, sherds of similar material from the same level were counted, labeled, and bagged.

Figure 4.11. Participants in the second excavation team.

5

Bioarchaeological Analysis of Remains

As noted earlier, only fragmentary skeletal remains were recovered. Given the early-twentieth-century history of the site, I assumed that most of the skeletal remains were gathered and disposed of elsewhere in preparation for constructing the sidewalk. I determined that the identifiable skeletal remains in the six units we excavated represented a minimum number of five adult individuals (Table 5.1). A sixth individual, a subadult, was represented by five teeth that were surface-collected from soil around the opening of one of several holes drilled across the western portion of the site.

Factors such as the construction of the sidewalk, an inexperienced field crew, and the compacted and moist sand meant that none of the larger bones were recovered in one piece. Consequently, it was not possible to make any of the statistical measurements that are used to determine the sex or age of the adult individuals. However, it was possible to examine the bones and teeth for evidence of pathologies. What follows are the summary assessments for each of the six sets of remains. Any assessment of these remains has only limited utility, since this collection of human skeletal remains is very small and is not representative of the site or of the historic community this cemetery served. Nevertheless, the presence of pathologies provides at least some insight on the lives of these individuals.

Test Unit

These remains consisted of an assortment of fragmented but recognizable bones. None of the bones include features that can be readily used to suggest sex. I noted no pathologies on any of these bones. However, the linea aspera (a ridge of roughened surface on the posterior surface of the femur

Table 5.1. Minimum number of individuals (MNI) for comingled remains from NP 250

Site #	Context	Element	Element ID	Side	%	Age	MNI
NP 250	Unit 2	Parietal		Left	> 75		1
NP 250	Unit 2	Parietal fragments		—	< 25		1
NP 250	Surface Find	Deciduous maxillary molar	1st	Left		Sub-adult	1
NP 250	Unit 4	Maxillary molar	1st	Right			1
NP 250	Unit 2	Clavicle		Left	> 75		1
NP 250	Unit 4	Clavicle		Left	25–75		1
NP 250	Unit 5	Clavicle		Left	<25		1
NP 250	Unit 1	Ribs	3rd–9th	Right	< 25		1
NP 250	Unit 2	Ribs	3rd–9th	Right	> 75, 25–75		1
NP 250	Test Unit	Radius		Right	< 25		1
NP 250	Unit 1	Radius		Right	25–75		1
NP 250	Unit 2	Ulna		Left	25–75		1
NP 250	Unit 4	Ulna		Left	25–75		1
NP 250	Test Unit	Phalanges—hand		Right	25–75, > 75		1
NP 250	Unit 1	Phalanges—hand		Right	25–75		1
NP 250	Surface Find	Thoracic vertebra	1st–9th		< 25		1
NP 250	Unit 2	Thoracic vertebrae	1st–9th		25–75, > 75		1
NP 250	Unit 4	Thoracic vertebra	1st–9th		< 25		1
NP 250	Unit 2	Lumbar vertebrae			25–75		1
NP 250	Unit 5	Lumbar vertebrae			< 25		1
NP 250	Test Unit	Phalanges—foot		Left	> 75		1
NP 250	Unit 2	Phalanges—foot		Left	> 75		1

to which muscles are attached) on the shaft of the left femur is fairly robust, which would suggest that this individual had a physically active lifestyle. This fragmentary example was the only identifiable femur recovered in this excavation. William Bass uses T. K. Black's technique of measuring the midshaft circumference of a femur to assess the sex of fragmentary examples (2005, 229–231). This is the method I used to assess this femur. While any measurement of this bone has no referent, even for this site, this ambiguity allows me to make the point that both men and women in this cemetery population would have engaged in physically demanding work. Therefore, it would be equally likely that this femur could have belonged to a woman or a man.

Unit 2, Levels 1 and 2

The largest number and variety of skeletal elements were recovered from this unit. After the team excavated an almost complete cranial vault in level 2, it became apparent that some of the cranial fragments previously discovered in level 1 represented at least one other individual. In level 2, the more complete cranial vault was found in association with much of a spinal column and a number of nonduplicated ribs. Based on this evidence, I assumed that these bones all represented elements from one individual. The cranial vault is incomplete and is missing features used for cranial measuring points and to estimate sex, such as the brow ridges and the muscle attachments (Bass 2005, 81). I interpreted a small filigree gold pin found in close association with the cranium as a pin for the neck of a woman's dress or blouse. Based on this evidence, I assumed that the individual buried with it was likely a female.

Some segments of the bone in this individual's cranial vault had thickened (7.74–10 millimeters). Thickening of cranial bone could be an indicator of some type of anemia that could have been the result of nutritional deficiency or disease (Khudabux 1999, 308; White 2000, 394). Other cranial bone fragments from the southern half of this unit were even thicker (11.60–13.49 millimeters). I have interpreted these fragments as belonging to another individual. It appears that anemia was chronic for this second individual. This health condition suggests that this person endured a life of nutritional imbalance due to limited options in food choices. An individual affected by anemia was quite likely to be affected by other nutritional deficiencies (Walker et al. 2009, 116).

The pitted surface of the bone in the small intact section of the left eye orbit is evidence of cribra orbitalia, another indicator of nutritional deficiency. This condition is often attributed to a diet deficient in animal foods rich in vitamin B_{12} and deficiency-related diseases such as scurvy and rickets (Khudabux 1999, 308; Walker et al. 2009, 115–116). These nutritional deficiencies can be further exacerbated by intestinal parasites, the transmission of which is facilitated by poor sanitation and a contaminated water supply (Walker et al. 2009, 118). The only other pathology noted from this excavation unit is dental caries (tooth decay) on the occlusal (top, or chewing) surface of one tooth, a second left upper molar (LM). These were the two largest cranial fragments identified, but they also are a very small sample. It is not possible to make any assertions from a sample this small apart from the fact that these two individuals evidently endured life conditions in which they were nutritionally challenged and possibly did not live in the most sanitary conditions. Given the low social status of both enslaved persons and free blacks, it was quite likely that most of the individuals buried in this cemetery endured a limited food supply and lived in congested neighborhoods with water wells dangerously close to pit latrines.

Units 4 and 5

Only small fragmented human bones were recovered from Units 4 and 5. No skeletal pathologies were noted for any of these remains. The bones from each of these units were estimated as representing the remains of at least one individual for each unit.

Surface Collections

A set of seven teeth were retrieved from the sand piled around the opening of one of the drilled holes. These teeth were determined to be those of a subadult about 10 to 11 years old (Bass 2005, 302). The group of teeth consisted of two incisors and five molars, including a deciduous left first molar and the unerupted crown of a third mandibular molar. The two incisors have transverse lines, an indication of enamel hypoplasia (White 2000, 526). Dental enamel hypoplasia is an indicator of "systemic metabolic stress associated with infectious disease [or] insufficient calcium, protein, or carbohydrates" (Blakey and Rankin-Hill 2009, 144). These were the only examples of lateral incisors excavated; the other incisors included one maxillary and one mandibular central incisor from Unit 4. The two lateral incisors were the only teeth impacted by enamel hypoplasia (Figure 5.1).

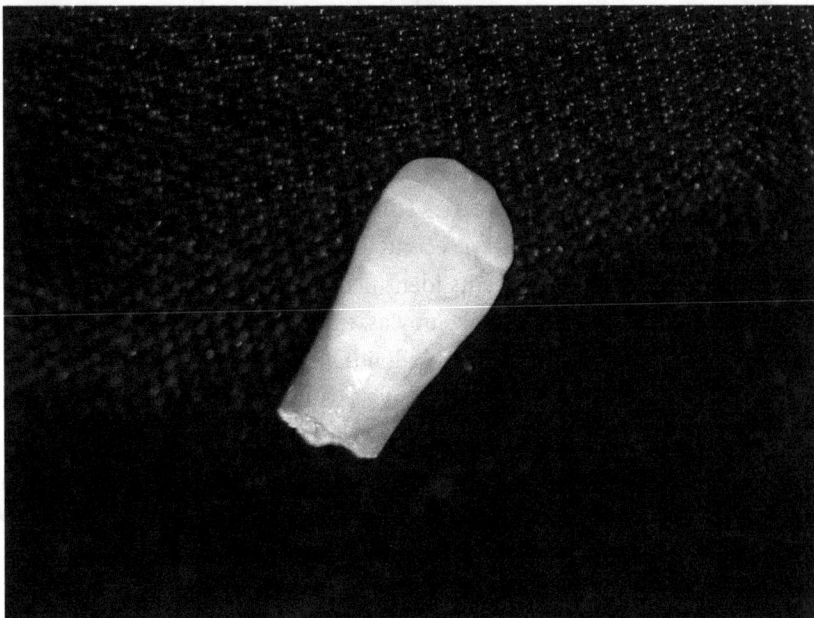

Figure 5.1. Enamel hypoplasia on a right upper lateral incisor.

This tiny sample cannot be assumed to be representative of the cemetery population or the affiliated communities.

These pathologies all raise questions about the possible extent to which the conditions they are indications of were evident among urban African-Bahamian communities, a population that likely lived on the economic margins of the wider society. Even in an urban environment where enslaved workers could work for hire and free blacks were independent workers, the economic opportunities for the black population were quite limited. Employment opportunities in Nassau for black men would have included work as a mariner or a fisherman or varied work on land associated with building and maintaining boats (Turner 2007, 4). The site retained evidence from the early twentieth century that suggests that the Northern Burial Ground site was used as an area of access for boats moored along the shore.

Black women in Nassau would have found work primarily as itinerant street vendors. They would have carried their wares in wide, shallow baskets balanced on their heads. Sources such as notices in the only eighteenth-century newspaper, *The Bahama Argus*, and depictions in nineteenth-century sources indicate that the street vendors who hawked cooked foodstuffs or fruits and vegetables were usually women. A public produce market was constructed in the 1790s on Bay Street opposite its junction with one of two streets leading into the city from the black neighborhood south of the hill at the city's southern limit. The only eighteenth-century account that referred to the everyday lives of blacks was recorded by Johann David Schoepf in *Travels in the Confederation, 1783–1784*. Schoepf was a German-born doctor who was also trained as a botanist and zoologist. He went to New York in 1777 to serve as chief surgeon for the Ansbach regiment of Hessian troops who were fighting for the British in the American Revolutionary War. Dr. Schoepf wanted to study the Americas as a scientist, so he traveled for two years through Philadelphia, Virginia, the Carolinas, British East Florida, and the Bahamas before returning to England. Schoepf was making his tour during the aftermath of the war, when Loyalist refugees were still migrating into the colony. His brief descriptions provide some insight into life in Nassau at a time when the Northern Burial Ground would have been in use:

> To the east of the town, along the waterside, are a good number of houses, for the most part occupied by sailors and fishermen; and several English miles farther on is a little village, to which the name New-Guinea has been given, most of its inhabitants being free negroes and mulattoes. . . . Even the blacks here take part in the general contentment. They are everywhere of a better appearance, breathing happiness; strong, well-fed, and of a decent demeanor. Many of them are free, or if they are slaves, by paying a small weekly sum they are left undisturbed in the enjoyment of what they gain by other work. Some of them own houses and plantations, and others are even put in command of small vessels. Fishing is a common employment of the poorer white inhabitants as well as of many negroes; however fish are not always to be had when wanted. (Schoepf 1911, 263–264, 276, 301)

Schoepf's comment has historical value because his observations are contemporary. However, his assessment of blacks in Nassau as being "strong, well-fed, and of a decent demeanor" was overly optimistic because he only observed these people from a distance that was filtered through factors such as race, class, and cultural background. Schoepf's rosy assessment contrasts with my limited archaeological assessment of that population. While the archaeological sample is too small to make any definitive statements about the daily lives of this historical population the contrast of my archaeological findings with Schoepf's statement is a reminder that contemporary statements written by persons who were not part of the community in question need to be weighed in relation to other potentially informative material, such as archaeological remains that were used and deposited by members of the community. There are limitations to both sources of information. In the absence of any other sources, then, the cautious insights that can be gleaned from this work is the extent of our knowledge of this historical black Bahamian community at this point.

The robust muscle attachment on the femur of one individual suggests physical exertion that would be consistent with the general lifestyle of a laborer. Other bone and dental pathologies indicate that those individuals faced nutritional deficiency as a result of poor nutrition, disease, or both. Though free and enslaved black men and women could create independent lives for themselves in Nassau, these remains are evidence of the fact that some still faced significant health challenges such as access to a nutritionally balanced diet and possibly poor sanitation.

6

Interpretations of Artifacts and Ecofacts

Because this site was subjected to multiple episodes of disturbance, the interpretation of archaeological evidence from the site must rely heavily on the cultural material excavated. Only a few contemporary accounts were written about the lives of these urban communities. Of the artifacts and ecofacts excavated, three material categories were selected for more detailed analysis because of the potential for such research to add layers of information about how the site was used. These three material categories were ceramic sherds, glass sherds, and faunal remains.

Other material categories were deemed less helpful for a number of reasons. Although many nails were excavated, I did not study them because they would require electrolytic conservation treatment. The artifact conservation facility in Nassau was set up to treat much larger iron objects such as cannons and cannon balls, not objects as small as nails. This was unfortunate. Techniques for manufacturing nails changed over time, and even though there is considerable time overlap for each variety, the presence of different styles of nail gives some idea of the general period of use (Nöel-Hume 1991, 252–254). Wherever conservation facilities make it possible, this loose chronology can provide an additional line of evidence with other datable cultural chronologies.

Quite a large amount of brick was also recovered. In the eighteenth and nineteenth centuries, gravesites were sometimes curbed using brick. The use of brick in curbing for graves suggests a significant financial outlay. Although it was useful to note the use of brick as an architectural feature for some gravesites, since the original context of the site has been destroyed, the research value of brick is limited to acknowledging its use to curb some graves in this cemetery. This detail in itself is quite significant since it suggests that for some grave sites in this cemetery there was a substantial cost; a detail worth noting for a community that was generally quite poor. Some shell and stone were also collected, but I interpreted them as elements of the Lucayan component of this site.

Ceramics

One of the African-derived grave treatments provided archaeological evidence for personal items placed on top of graves. Ethnographic and folklore research in the Bahamas and elsewhere in the Americas suggest that ceramic vessels are commonly part of displays of personal belongings on graves. These included plates, bowls, pans, tea wares (cups and saucers), and stoneware bottles. Even though the site's original context has been destroyed, archaeological investigation proceeded on the assumption that cultural materials excavated within this site were likely related to its use over time as a cemetery for people of African descent. The exceptions were objects that were likely deposited within the site after it was no longer used as a cemetery.

Apart from being the largest category of cultural material, the excavated ceramics proved to also be the most chronologically informative cultural material. Establishing a timeline for cultural activity within this cemetery space relied most heavily on the period of manufacture for the variety of ceramic types that were excavated. In reviewing the manufacturing dates for ceramic types that were identified, two unanticipated patterns became evident. First, a number of ceramic types (62 percent) were first manufactured before 1770. Second, only a few (5 percent) of the identified ceramic types were manufactured after 1840. About 8 percent of the ceramics excavated date to the second half of the twentieth century; these were interpreted as having been deposited within the site long after it had been used as a cemetery (see Table 6.2).

This first finding caused a rethinking of the chronology for this site. What if the Northern Burial Ground was established in the first half of the eighteenth century, as was Centre Burial Ground across the street? If these two cemeteries both dated to the early 1700s, then their location on opposite sides of the street was likely not coincidental. Further, what if the Northern Burial Ground always met the needs of an African-descended population? If that were the case, then this cemetery was established by a local black community to satisfy their preferred cultural needs for memorializing their dead. These new questions challenged the presumption that the Northern Burial Ground was established in the late 1700s as part of the more rigidly enforced racially segregated social order introduced by Loyalist immigrants from the former American colonies, as archival documents recording the cemetery's consecration suggested.

The second finding from the relative dating indicated that only one ceramic type represented in the excavated materials had a date of first manufacture after 1840. Since documentary records show that the cemetery was maintained until the early twentieth century and was presumably in continued use until then, the expectation was that there would be more examples and a wider variety of ceramic types that were manufactured in the second half of the nineteenth century. That there were so few identified ceramic types from the mid-nineteenth century and later suggested that the cultural practice of leaving ceramic vessels on top of graves had been discontinued by the mid-nineteenth century. If this was so, then it would be a significant change in a cultural practice that had continued within this cemetery space for about 100 years before that time and had likely factored into the rationale for establishing this separate cemetery space. What kinds of social issues could initiate such changes?

Chronologically informative evidence derived from the bottle glass and faunal remains all seemed to reinforce the general trend seen for the ceramics. What follows is a synopsis of the types of ceramics represented from the site's history as a cemetery. These are listed in chronological order for the earliest period these wares would have been on the market:

Tin-Glazed Ware—Polychrome: 1571–1790

Tin-glazed wares were the prevalent European ceramic type for over 200 years, from the sixteenth through the eighteenth centuries. British colonies such as the Bahamas usually had Dutch- or English-made tin-glazed products. The more colorful styles can date as early as the sixteenth century but remained on the market until the late eighteenth century, when creamware became more popular. Only a few small sherds were recovered at this site, which suggests that tin-glazed ware could represent a use period for this cemetery that was earlier than the late eighteenth century (Figure 6.1). Ceramic forms in this style from this site were all plates.[1]

Tin-Glazed Ware, Blue on White: 1630–1790

Tin-glazed ceramics with hand-painted decorations in cobalt blue were common through much of the seventeenth and eighteenth centuries. Different design motifs were prevalent during particular periods. The design motifs

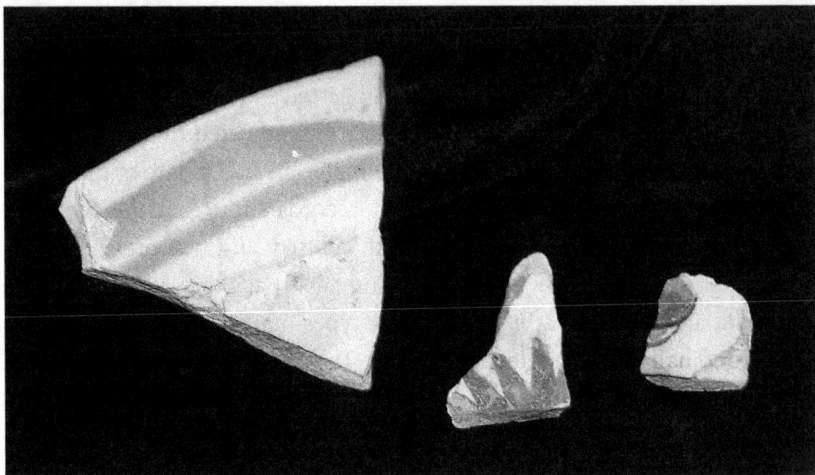

Figure 6.1. Selection of polychrome painted decoration on tin-glazed ware.

recovered from the Northern Burial Ground site were oriental-style land-scapes with a general timeline of 1671–1788 and Chinese floral patterns with a general timeline of 1669–1793 (Figure 6.2). Although these patterns were still available in the late eighteenth century, they could have been placed in the cemetery at some earlier point in the eighteenth century since these designs were popular for such a long time.[2] Sherds of this ceramic type represent several forms that include plates, rimmed plates, and bowls.

Staffordshire-Type Slipware: 1675–1770

By the late seventeenth century, Staffordshire-type slipware featured predominantly utilitarian forms. Design techniques included trailing a dark-colored slip over a white background. The lead glaze used to finish such pieces gives them the distinctive colors of yellow and shades of brown. Hollow forms such as cups, bowls, and jugs were often also decorated with dots near the rim. The rim of large flat forms such as chargers, plates, and milk pans were often crimped to form pie crust–like impressions as a finish for the rim. This type of ceramic was not exported across the Atlantic after about 1770, so this ware type represents an eighteenth-century period of use (Figure 6.3). Forms of Staffordshire-type slipware recovered from this site included some hollow forms such as a cup, mug, or jug; plates; and milk pans (a large, flat dish with sloping or upright sides like a pie pan).[3]

Figure 6.2. Hand-painted designs on tin-glazed blue on white sherds.

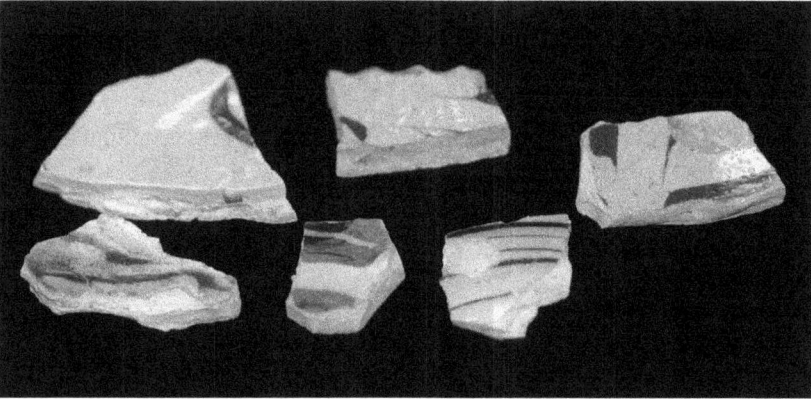

Figure 6.3. Slipware with trailed, combed, and marbled designs.

Manganese Mottled Ware: 1675–1780

The most common form of this type of ceramic is drinking vessels such as tankards, mugs, and cups. Cordoned bands near the rim and the base were the decorative technique used most often on these containers. Only one small sherd was recovered at the Northern Burial Ground site (Figure 6.4). Although it is quite possible that this vessel belonged to someone who was buried here in this cemetery in the late eighteenth century or even in the

Figure 6.4. Manganese Mottled ware sherd with cordoned lines.

early nineteenth century, it is also possible that this vessel was originally placed on a grave here earlier in the eighteenth century.[4]

Fulham-Type Stoneware: 1675–1775

This stoneware type was developed in the last quarter of the seventeenth century in imitation of Rhenish brown stoneware from the Rhineland region that is now part of Germany. Although this ware type was developed by a potter in Fulham, it is now also referred to as English brown stoneware since it was made in other places besides Fulham. Drinking vessels such as mugs and tankards and bottles were the most common forms of this type of ceramic, but a variety of other forms were also made, including jugs, jars, bowls, and coffee and tea services.[5] A total of five small sherds was excavated; these fit together in two larger fragments. This is another ceramic type that could indicate an earlier use of this property as a cemetery.

North Devon Gravel-Tempered Ware: 1680–1750

This was a utilitarian ceramic type that was in use mainly to the mid-eighteenth century. Pieces of this ware type were often undecorated. The most common forms were milk pans and butter pots.[6] This sherd is possibly from a milk pan (Figure 6.5). This one sherd indicates that this site may have been used as a cemetery by African-descended people well before Loyalist refugees moved to the Bahamas in the 1780s.

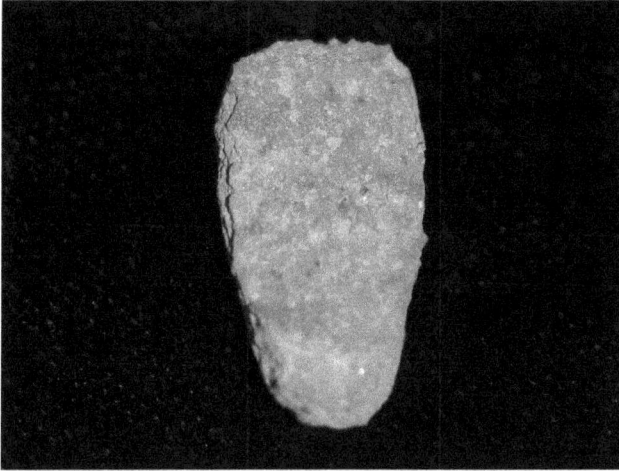

Figure 6.5. North Devon Gravel-tempered ceramic, mid-eighteenth century.

Nottingham Stoneware: 1700–1810

This type of ceramic was produced throughout the eighteenth century, although it was manufactured in less quantity after about 1775. Only hollow vessel forms such as tankards, cups, mugs, pitchers, punch bowls, tea, and coffee pots were produced in Nottingham stoneware. Decorative techniques on these forms included incised or engine-turned rouletting or cordoned bands, sprig-molded appliqués, and a variety of hand-finished decorations.[7] This was the only sherd of Nottingham stoneware recovered (Figure 6.6). It is likely from a drinking vessel such as a mug, a cup, or a tankard. The rouletting suggests that this fragment was near the rim of the vessel. A container for drinking would be consistent with the African-derived custom of placing personal food containers on the top of a gravesite.

Astbury Type: 1720–1750

Also sometimes referred to as simply fine red earthenware, this type of ceramic was used mainly for tea wares such as teapots, tea cups, bowls, and coffee pots. These forms were often decorated with bands of white pipe clay slip near the rim and sprig-molded appliqués in a variety of forms such as animals, flowers, and royal coats of arms.[8] This tiny rim sherd was part of some hollow form, likely a cup or a bowl. Because the end manufacture date for this type of ceramic is in the mid-eighteenth century, its presence

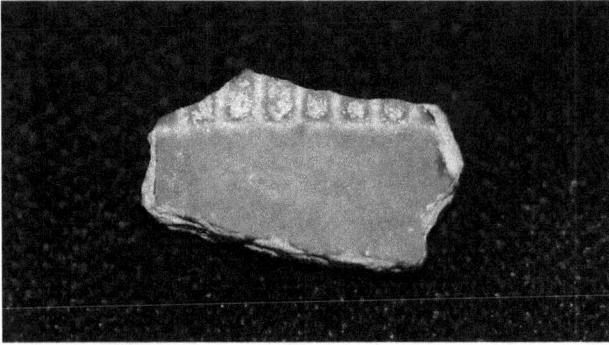

Figure 6.6. Nottingham Stoneware sherd with rouletting decoration.

adds to the hypothesis that this cemetery predated the late-eighteenth-century Loyalist migration.

Chinese Porcelain: 1700–1810

Chinese porcelain in the Americas likely dates from one of two dynasties: the Ming Dynasty (1364–1644) or the Ch'ing Dynasty (1644–1912). A mark identifying the reign when a piece was manufactured would serve as an important chronological indicator. However, during the eighteenth century, Chinese export porcelain decorated in blue underglaze almost never had reign marks. This makes it very difficult to reliably date even complete pieces.

In archaeological sites where ceramics are most often recovered as relatively small sherds, archaeologists often have to rely on such tangential evidence as change over time in decorative styles and techniques. None of the porcelain sherds excavated from the Northern Burial Ground site appear to fit the general description of late-eighteenth- to early-nineteenth-century Chinese porcelain from Canton or Nanking, which is characterized by coarsely executed designs done in intense cobalt blue. Based on the absence of these decorative elements, it is possible that these porcelain sherds date to earlier than the late 1700s. As the eighteenth century progressed, Chinese porcelain became more affordable, and by the mid-eighteenth century, Chinese porcelain was present in many places (Figure 6.7). The significance of factoring in Chinese porcelain for this site is that it helps illustrate the great variety of ceramic types that was available to Nassau's urban black communities.[9]

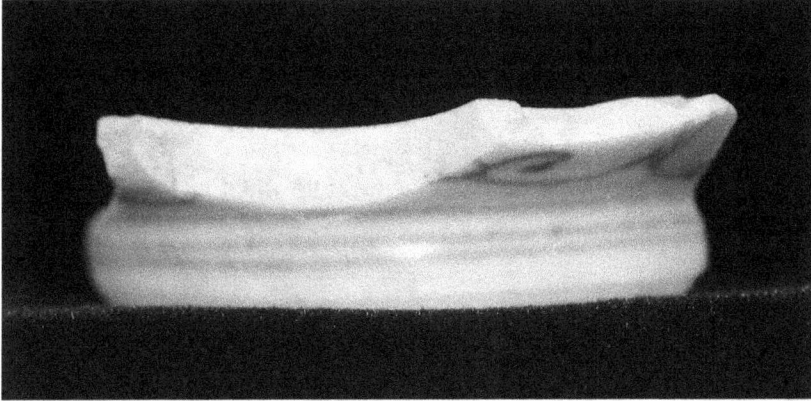

Figure 6.7. Base of a porcelain tea bowl imported from China.

Buckley-Type Stoneware: 1720–1820

This ware type used a combination of red and yellowish clays. The result was a paste that ranged from brick-red to a dark, purplish color. Finished articles were covered with a heavy glaze that could range in color from black to a lighter brown. Vessels of this ware type included table wares such as cups, bowls, and pitchers and utilitarian vessels such as storage jars, milk pans, and cooking pots. These articles were usually not decorated. Only storage vessels were glazed on both surfaces; all others were glazed only on the interior surface.[10] Two sherds of this ware type were excavated at this site.

Scratch Blue Salt-Glazed Stoneware: 1735–1775

The decorative technique is the distinguishing feature of this variety of salt-glazed stoneware. Incised geometric and floral patterns were infilled with blue-colored cobalt oxide. Any excess pigment was wiped away, leaving color only within the incised designs. This ware type included tea wares, pitchers, punch pots, and loving cups.[11] Two sherds were excavated; both represent hollow forms. The very thin rim sherd could have been part of a tea bowl, while the heavier base sherd could have been part of a pitcher, a tankard, or a loving cup (Figure 6.8). As with the other type of white salt-glazed stoneware, this scratch blue ceramic could have been placed in this cemetery sometime before the 1780s. Although this ware type was not manufactured after about 1775, pieces were likely still in use some fifteen to twenty years after that.

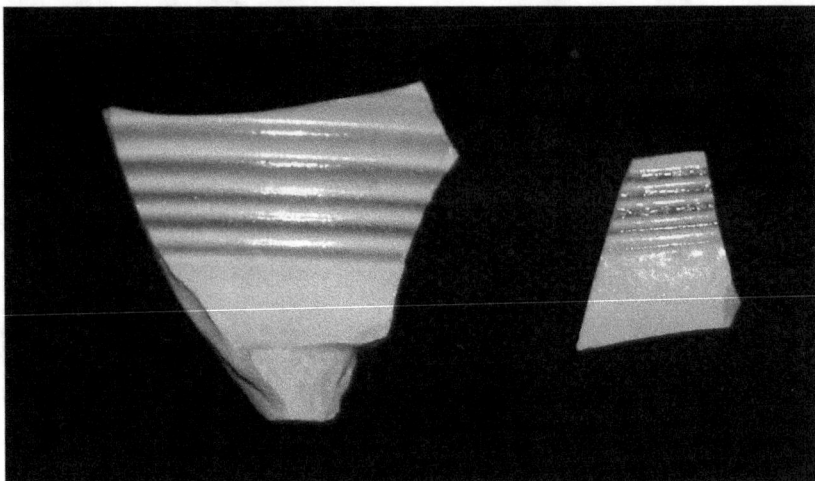

Figure 6.8. Scratch blue salt-glazed sherds.

Press-Molded White Salt-Glazed Stoneware: 1740–1770

This is a thinly potted, white-bodied, salt-glazed stoneware that was developed with the inclusion of calcined flint about 1720. This revised manufacturing process further refined an earlier type of white-bodied English stoneware. The forms manufactured using this technique included table wares such as tea wares, jugs, mugs, pitchers, and tankards.

By 1740 block press–molded and slip-cast decorative forms had become the most common forms of English white salt-glazed stoneware. Press-molded designs included barleycorn; dot, diaper, and basket; and bead and reel. This ceramic type was popular due in part to its modest cost. However, the popularity of white salt-glazed stoneware was eventually superseded by creamware.[12] The press-molded decorated sherds that were excavated from this site all appear to be various kinds of plates (Figure 6.9). The manufacturing dates for this ceramic style add to speculation that this cemetery site predated the establishment of the Northern Burial Ground in the late eighteenth century.

Stoneware Mineral Water Bottle: Circa 1750–1760

Research on this stoneware sherd proved rather difficult; I could find nothing similar in any reference books. The mystery was solved with a visit to

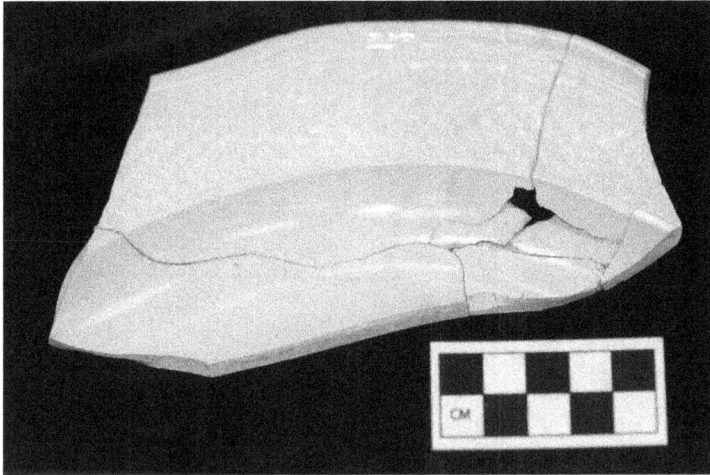

Figure 6.9. Portion of a white salt-glazed rimmed plate.

the DeWitt Wallace Museum in Colonial Williamsburg. An exhibit there on stoneware in colonial America, *Pottery with a Past*, included a similar stoneware bottle. It was made in Westerwald, Germany, to hold mineral water, an expensive health fad of the mid-eighteenth century (Skerry and Hood 2010) that lasted for only about a decade. The characteristic feature of these bottles is an incised label on the shoulder that could also be encircled by a ring of cobalt blue color (Figure 6.10). Finds such as this bottle suggest that at least some members of this community were able to participate in contemporary trends in material culture.

American Coarse Redware: 1750–1820

This utilitarian ceramic type was made in North America initially by German immigrant potters in Pennsylvania, New England, and North Carolina. The main decorative technique involved trailing white slip onto a piece in simple geometric bands, stripes, loops, or lobes and then covered them with a clear lead glaze on the interior surface only. Common food-related forms manufactured in this ceramic style included platters, plates, saucers, bowls, milk pans, teapots, jars, jugs, and pitchers.[13] Sherds excavated from this site all appear to have been part of a flat open form such as a milk pan (Figure 6.11). Manufacturing dates for this ceramic style would fit with a late-eighteenth-century use of this cemetery.

Figure 6.10. Partial incised label on a mineral water bottle.

Figure 6.11. American Coarse Redware rim sherd.

Clouded or Tortoiseshell Wares: 1750–1770

A cream-bodied refined earthenware was developed in England around 1740. Manufacturers experimented with adding various colored metal oxides to the glazes that were applied to this cream-bodied ceramic, resulting in mottled patterns in purple, blue, brown, yellow, green, and gray. This ceramic type is sometimes called Whieldon ware, after the primary devel-

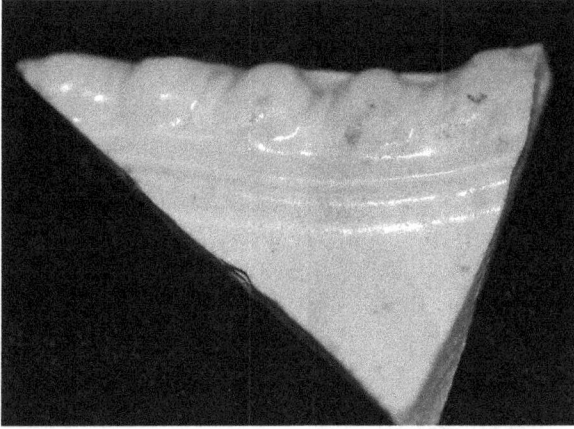

Figure 6.12. Creamware plate with molded rim pattern.

oper of this ceramic style, but it is also known as clouded or tortoiseshell ware because it was produced by many potteries.[14] Just one tiny sherd of tortoiseshell-style ceramic was excavated at the Northern Burial Ground site. This is another example of a mid-eighteenth-century ware type that raises the possibility of an earlier use period for the site.

Creamware: 1762–1820

In 1762, Josiah Wedgwood introduced a clear lead-glazed cream-colored ceramic he called creamware. Wedgwood adapted a white salt-glazed rim pattern for his signature creamware designs that was called Queen's ware and the Royal pattern. This new ceramic type contributed to the decline of earlier ware types such as white salt-glazed stoneware and tin-glazed enamel wares (Figure 6.12). A new pattern known as feather edge was produced from 1765 to about 1810.[15]

Pearlware: 1775–1840

Just as creamware eclipsed white salt-glazed stoneware and tin-glazed enamel wares as the most popular ceramic ware, so pearlware eclipsed creamware. Pearlware remained the prevalent type of affordable refined earthenware for about sixty years. During this time, technological developments allowed manufacturers to test the public appeal of a number of decorative techniques. Marbleized pearlware, the style shown in Figure

Figure 6.13. A pearlware
sherd with marbleized
decoration.

6.13, was manufactured from 1782 to about 1820 (Figure 6.13). Vessel forms
in the various styles of this ware type included tea wares, plates, platters,
and bowls.[16]

American Stoneware: 1780–1890

This ware type was developed by the late eighteenth century to replace Ger-
man-made stonewares. American stoneware vessels were thicker than similar German forms. The most common forms of this heavy-duty utilitarian
ware were jugs that were used as storage for a variety of liquids. Decorative
motifs were executed free hand or were stenciled in cobalt. Details such as
the volume of the container and business labels were stamped into the body
of the vessel.[17] The few sherds that were excavated at the Northern Burial
Ground all represent these large storage jar forms.

White Ware: 1830–

White ware eventually replaced pearlware as the most popular and affordable
ware type. Hand-painted and sponged designs were most popular until the
1840s. This is the first ware type excavated from this site that was developed
in the nineteenth century (Figure 6.14). White granite, or ironstone, china
was first patented about 1813 but did not become more common until about
1840. This utilitarian ware type had a dense, semi-vitrified paste. Design motifs on white granite were usually molded into the piece; overglaze decorative
elements in metallic luster finish were sometimes added.[18]

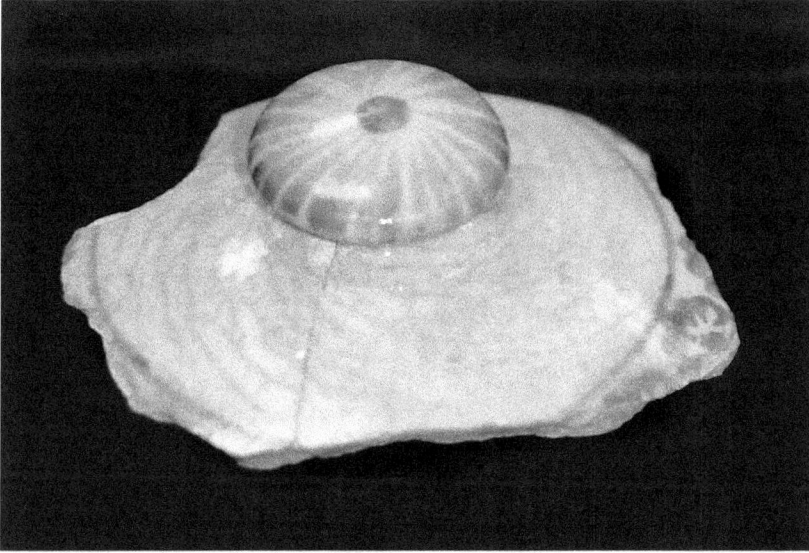

Figure 6.14. Reconstructed lid of a white ware container.

Guanajuato Majolica: 1850–1900

This ceramic type was manufactured in Mexico. It was a utilitarian ware covered in a thick enamel layer over a hard, compact paste core. Decoration consisted of hand-painted floral motifs in orange, green, yellow, purple, blue, brown, and black. The usual forms manufactured included cups, bowls, and plates.[19] One sherd of this ceramic type was excavated at the Northern Burial Ground site. It was identified as Guanajuato polychrome type majolica based on the distinctive emerald green color used on this ceramic (Figure 6.15). It is unusual to find this Hispanic ceramic type in this British colony. I have interpreted it as evidence that black Bahamian workers took advantage of wage-earning opportunities around the region in the late nineteenth century after emancipation in the United States in 1865 and in Cuba in 1886.

Whiteware Manufactured by W. H. Grindley & Co.: 1936–1954

This pottery was established in 1880 by William Harry Grindley at the Newfield Pottery in Tunstall, Stoke-on-Trent. The company manufactured earthenware and ironstone china that was exported predominantly to mar-

Figure 6.15. Floral motif on a sherd of Guanajuato Majolica.

Figure 6.16. Partial maker's mark of W. H. Grindley & Co.

kets in Canada, the United States, South America, and Australia. (Birks n.d.). The three sherds excavated from the Northern Burial Ground site display the company's logo, which was used from about 1936 to 1954 (Figure 6.16). Based on what is known of the history of this site, these dates suggest the vessel was likely deposited on the site when some iteration of the sidewalk was being constructed.

Evaluation

The consistent presence of ceramic types with end manufacturing dates that do not overlap with the Loyalist migration into the Bahamas raised questions about whether this cemetery was first established in the 1790s, as the consecration document indicated. Additional factors such as a history of free black settlements in this area and the location of this site adjacent to an earlier cemetery suggest that this cemetery was already a deliberately constructed African-influenced cemetery space before the late eighteenth century. If that were the case, it would make a compelling argument for the level of cultural agency that both enslaved and freed Africans and their descendants were able to exert well before any Loyalists arrived.

Despite the fact that this is a disturbed site, the analysis of ceramic types demonstrated a number of issues relevant to an understanding of the community that used this property as a cemetery for possibly almost two centuries. To begin with, the inventory in this chapter gives some idea of the variety of ceramic types that were available to the urban black population of Nassau in the eighteenth and nineteenth centuries. The list of over twenty ceramic types represents only those that could be reliably identified (Table 6.1). Because not all of these ceramics were lower-cost utilitarian wares, this array of material culture counters the assumption that the low status of the associated community would be reflected in low-cost and, presumably, low-quality material items.

Minimum vessel counts of these ceramic types show that some 84 percent of the wares identified were manufactured during the eighteenth and into the early nineteenth centuries (Table 6.2). These statistics indicate that the customary placement of ceramics on graves was most frequent during the eighteenth century and continued through the first half of the nineteenth century; after which the placement of ceramic tableware on graves apparently declined sharply. Considering the minimum number of ceramic vessels that had beginning manufacture dates earlier than 1770 (55 of 89 examples, or 62 percent) it is plausible that this site was in use before the 1780s or 1790s.

The number of sherds and the variety of ceramic types represented at this site suggest a history of use that is consistent with the African-derived cultural practice of leaving eating and drinking vessels on top of graves. The periods of manufacture for the ceramics especially suggest that this cultural practice continued in this cemetery for much of the period it was in use. That remnants of these ceramics still remain on this site suggests these personal items on tops of graves remained as a feature

Table 6.1. Frequency of datable ceramic types

Ceramic Type	Date of Manufacture	# Sherds
Tin-glazed enamel	1571–1790	1
Tin-glazed enamel	1630–1790	36
Staffordshire slipware	1675–1770	13
Manganese Mottled ware	1675–1780	1
North Devon gravel-tempered	1680–1750	1
Chinese porcelain	1680–1750	6
English brown stoneware	1690–1800	1
Nottingham stoneware	1700–1810	1
Astbury	1720–1750	1
White salt-glazed stoneware	1720–1770	2
White salt-glazed stoneware	1735–1775	5
White salt-glazed stoneware	1740–1790	2
White salt-glazed stoneware	1750–1780	11
Scratch blue salt-glazed stoneware	1735–1775	3
Creamware	1750–1770	1
Creamware	1765–1810	1
Creamware	1762–1820	18
Pearlware	1775–1810	1
Pearlware	1775–1840	14
Pearlware	1780–1840	5
Pearlware	1782–1820	1
Pearlware	1795–1820	2
Pearlware	1802–1846	1
Pearlware	1830–1840	1
Coarse redware	18th century	2
Salt-glazed stoneware	1750s–	3
North American redware	1750–1820	5
American stoneware	1780–1890	8
Whiteware	1820–1860	14
Whiteware	1830–20th century	18
Yellow ware	1840–20th century	1
Majolica: Guanajuato	1850–1900	1

Ceramic Type	Date of Manufacture	# Sherds
Opal glass or milk glass	1880–1940	1
Lead-glazed redware	18th century	1
Stoneware	19th century	1
Porcelaneous material	19th century	1
Refined redware	19th century	1
West Indian stoneware	19th century	1
American brown stoneware	19th century	2
Unidentified stoneware	19th century	1
Refined ceramic	1960–	2
Refined ceramic	1990s–	1
Coarse ceramic	20th century	8
Terra-cotta	20th century	3
Refined ceramic	20th century	3
Plastic	20th century	1

of an African-derived cemetery landscape even after the cemetery was no longer in use. It is likely not a mere coincidence that the Northern Burial Ground is situated across the street from Centre Burial Ground, the earliest surviving cemetery in Nassau. The earliest dates on headstones in Centre Burial Ground cemetery indicate that it dates at least to the 1730s and possibly as early as the 1720s, when the government of the colony was finally revived after the Bahamas had served for several decades as a haven for pirates.

In addition, the ceramic forms identified are all table and tea wares such as plates, saucers, bowls, cups, mugs, tankards, and teapots. People of African descent likely did not use these vessels in the same ways the European manufacturers intended. Such is the case with the milk pans; excavated remains of this kind of vessel were decorated as Staffordshire-type slipware. These vessels were left on top of graves like other food containers, suggesting that within this African-descended community these vessels were treated as a tableware from which food was eaten. Also represented are a variety of stoneware bottles and large jugs. The varieties of ceramic types from this site are indicative of general changes in manufacturing and consumption trends

Table 6.2. Inventory and description of ceramics

Ceramics—NP 250

Ceramic Type	Design	Vessel Part	Vessel Type	Date Manufactured	# Sherds	Unit	MNV	Notes
White salt-glazed stoneware	Barleycorn	Rim to base	Plate	1750–1780	11	Test Unit (TU)	1	About ⅓ of plate; glued
White salt-glazed stoneware		Rim	Tea bowl (?)	1740–1790	1	TU	1	Hollow form—very thin; possibly cup or small bowl
White salt-glazed stoneware	Bead and reel	Rim	Plate	1750–1775	1	TU	1	
Creamware		Base; base	Tea bowl	1762–1820	2	TU	1	
Creamware	Featheredge	Rim	Plate	1765–1810	1	TU	1	
Creamware		Body	Hollow form	1762–1820	3	TU	1	
Tin-glazed	Handpainted—blue	Body	Hollow form	1630–1790	8	TU	1	Painted under glaze
Tin-glazed	Handpainted	Rim	Bowl	1630–1790	1	TU	1	Ovoid shapes and dots within 2 lines; paste: peach color
Tin-glazed	Handpainted	Body; base	Plate	1630–1790	4	TU	1	
Tin-glazed	Handpainted	Rim	Bowl	1630–1790	1	TU	1	Single line below rim above floral design
Pearlware	Shell edge	Rim	Plate	1780–1840	4	TU	1	
Pearlware	Handpainted	Rim	Tea bowl	1830–1840	1	TU	1	Polychrome hand-painted pearlware (Florida Museum of Natural History)
Pearlware	Spattered and cordoned	Body	Tea bowl	1780–1840	1	TU	1	Hollow form—likely a tea bowl
Whiteware	Handpainted	Body	Plate	1830–present	2	TU	1	Sprig; painted patterns popular ca. 1840 (Florida Museum of Natural History)
Pearlware	Marbleized	Body	Bowl	1782–1820	1	TU	1	

Staffordshire-type slipware	Trailed and combed	Rim; body	Platter	1675–1770	2	TU	1	Crimped rim; peach-colored paste with inclusions
Staffordshire-type slipware	Combed	Body	Bowl	1675–1770	4	TU	1	Dark-brown combed lines; buff-colored paste
Staffordshire-type slipware	Trailed design	Body	Platter	1675–1770	1	TU	1	Caramel and dark-brown slip; peach-colored paste with no inclusions
Chinese porcelain		Body	Tea bowl	1644–1912	1	TU	1	Produced in the Qing Dynasty
Whiteware		Rim	Hollow form	1830–present	1	TU	1	
Creamware	Molded basketweave	Body	Bowl	1750–1770	1	TU	1	1750s–1770s: rococo-style ceramics emphasized naturalistic designs (DeWitt Wallace Decorative Arts Museum, Williamsburg, Va.)
Whiteware	Translucent green glaze	Base	Plate (?)	1830–present	3	TU	1	Glued; maker's mark: Grindley/England
Stoneware		Body	Jug	?	1	TU	1	Light-gray exterior with buff-colored interior glaze
Porcelaneous material		Base	Hollow form	?	1	TU	1	
Refined redware		Body; base	Tile	?	1	TU	1	One surface covered in lime mortar; possible grave decoration?
Salt-glazed stoneware	Incised label in cobalt blue	Shoulder; body	Bottle	1750s	3	TU	1	Mineral water bottle; Westerwald region, Germany
Staffordshire-type slipware	Lines near rim	Rim	Dish	1675–1770	1	TU	1	Glazed on rim and interior only
North American redware	Lead-glazed	Rim	Dish	1750–1820	1	TU	1	Rim turned out; glazed on interior only
North American redware	Slipped pattern	Body	Dish or bowl	1750–1820	4	TU	1	Dark-brown glaze with yellow slip pattern; only interior glazed
Stoneware	Dark-brown glaze	Base	Jug (?)	?	1	TU	1	Interior glaze
Tin-glazed		Rim	Mug or cup	1630–1790	1	1	1	Thin—undecorated

continued

Table 6.2.—*continued*

Ceramic Type	Design	Vessel Part	Vessel Type	Date Manufactured	# Sherds	Unit	MNV	Notes
Tin-glazed	Polychrome	Rim	Plate	1630–1790	1	1	1	Blue floral design with green leaves and outlined in black
Tin-glazed	Green on white	Rim	Plate	1630–1790	1	1	1	Double hand-painted lines around the marley
Tin-glazed	Blue on white	Rim to base	Plate	1630–1790	3	1	1	Hand-painted floral design
Tin-glazed	Blue on white	Rim; body	Bowl	1630–1790	8	1	1	Hand-painted exterior floral design; 2 filiate lines below rim
Scratch blue salt-glazed stoneware	Cordoned with blue	Body near base	Tankard or mug	1735–1775	1	1	1	
Scratch blue		Body	Cup	1735–1775	1	1	1	Very thin; delicate
White salt-glazed stoneware		Rim; body	Hollow form	1735–1775	5	1	1	Possibly from a tea bowl or caddy
Staffordshire-type slipware	Jeweled	Rim; handle; base	Bowl; or pitcher	1675–1770	2	1	1	Rim curled out; dots painted near rim
Creamware		Body	Tea bowl	1762–1820	1	1	1	Very thin and delicate
Creamware		Rim; body	Bowl or jug	1762–1820	3	1	1	Flattened top surface
Creamware		Body	Bowl	1762–1820	1	1	1	Thinner than previous 2 sherds
Creamware	Tortoiseshell; clouded	Body	Tea bowl or saucer	1750–1770	1	1	1	
Chinese porcelain	Blue/white floral	Base	Tea bowl	1644–1912	1	1	1	Very small sherd
Chinese porcelain	Blue/white floral	Base	Plate or saucer	1644–1912	1	1	1	
Pearlware	Polychrome floral	Rim; body	Tea bowl	1795–1820	2	1	1	Pattern near rim on interior and exterior surfaces
Pearlware	Shell edge	Rim (tiny flake)	Plate	1775–1840	1	1	1	
Pearlware		Spout; body	Teapot	1775–1840	1	1	1	

Ware	Decoration	Part	Vessel form	Date				Comments
Pearlware	Blue/white filigree	Handle—delicate	Tea cup	1775–1840	1	1	1	
Pearlware		Rim; body	Pitcher or jug	1775–1840	2	1	1	Appears to have been burned after deposition at this site
Whiteware		Body	Hollow form	1830–present	4	1	1	No exterior glaze; eroded green glaze; possibly Mexican majolica
Majolica—Guanajuato	Floral motif—green	Base	Plate or dish	1850–1900	1	1	1	Modern tile fragment
Refined ceramic		Body	Tile	ca. 1960 –	1	1	1	
Tin-glazed	Polychrome	Body	Plate	1571–1790	1	2	1	Floral design
Tin-glazed	Blue on white	Rim; body; base	Bowl	1630–1790	7	2	1	Hand painted on interior and exterior surfaces
North Devon gravel-tempered		Body	Bowl	1680–1750	1	2	1	Small sherd
White salt-glazed stoneware	Dot; diaper; basket	Rim	Plate	1720–1770	1	2	1	
White salt-glazed stoneware		Base	Hollow form	1720–1770	1	2	1	
Scratch blue	Cordoned lines—blue	Body	Tea bowl	1735–1775	1	2	1	Small, thin sherd
Nottingham stoneware	Rouletted	Body	Hollow form	1700–1810	1	2	1	
Astbury		Rim	Hollow form	1720–1750	1	2	1	Small sherd
Creamware		Base	Plate	1762–1820	1	2	1	
Staffordshire-type slipware	Marbled slip	Body; base	Dish or platter	1675–1770	2	2	1	
Pearlware	Polychrome	Spout	Coffee or chocolate pot	1775–1840	2	2	1	
Terra-cotta		Rim	Flower pot	20th century	1	2	1	
Whiteware	Metallic rim finish	Rim	Bowl	1860–20th century	8	2	1	

continued

Table 6.2.—*continued*

Ceramic Type	Design	Vessel Part	Vessel Type	Date Manufactured	# Sherds	Unit	MNV	Notes
Refined ceramic		Corner edge	Tile	ca. 1960–present	1	2	1	
Coarse ceramic		Rim; body	Drainage pipe	20th century	1	2	1	
Refined ceramic		Body	Hollow form	?	1	1	1	Wheel-thrown; unglazed; very lightweight
Coarse redware	Mottled glaze	Body; base	Dish or platter	Early 18th century	2	4	1	Lead-glazed interior; dark brown and yellowish-green glaze
Unidentified stoneware		Body	Storage jar	?	1	4	1	Eroded glaze on exterior surface
Staffordshire-type slipware		Rim	Hollow form	1675–1770	1	4	1	
Manganese Mottled ware	Cordoned	Body	Tankard or mug	1675–1780	1	4	1	Also called Mottled ware; Staffordshire Mottled; Staffordshire tortoise shell lead-glazed
Chinese porcelain	Blue under glaze	Rim	Hollow form	1644–1912	2	4	1	Likely some form of tea ware
Creamware		Rim	Plate	1762–1820	2	4	1	
Creamware		Rim; body; base	bowl	1762–1820	3	4	1	
Pearlware	Shell edge	Rim; base	Plate	1775–1840	3	4	1	
Pearlware	Blue under glaze	Rim	Tea bowl	1775–1810	2	4	1	Date based on design technique used[a]
Pearlware	Sponged—green	Body and spout (?)	Hollow form	1775–1840	1	4	1	This type sponge decoration was most popular in 1830s[a]
Yellow ware		Body	Hollow form	1840–20th century	2	4	1	
American stoneware	Blue on gray	Body	Jug or storage jar	1780–1890	6	4	1	

Type	Decoration/Glaze	Part	Form	Date				Notes
American stoneware	Bristol glaze	Base	Storage jar or jug	?	1	4	1	Interior and exterior glaze
Opal glass or milk glass	Press molded	Body		1880–1940	1	4	1	
Terra-cotta		Body	Tile	?	3	4	1	Lime mortar on bottom surface
Refined ceramic	Enameled glaze	Body	Tile (complete)	ca.1960–present	1	4	1	
Refined ceramic		Body	Tile	ca. 1960–present	7	4	7	3 complete tiles; 4 fragments of an oblong black tile with a matte finish
Coarse ceramic		Body	Drainage pipe	20th c	1	4	1	Similar to a fragment from Unit 2
Tin-glazed		Base	Plate	1630–1790	1	5	1	
Lead-glazed redware	Marbled glaze	Base	Dish or platter	18th century	1	5	1	
English brown stoneware		Body	Jug or storage jar	ca. 1690–1775	2	5	1	Also known as Fulham-type stoneware
Luster ware	High gloss finish	Body	Jug or storage jar	1815–1860s	1	5	1	
Chinese porcelain	Blue under glaze	Base with foot ring	Tea bowl	1644–1912	1	5	1	
Creamware		Body		1762–1820	1	5	1	Tiny sherd
Pearlware	Shell edge	Rim; base	Plate	1775–1840	2	5	1	
Pearlware	Transfer printed—blue	Rim	Teacup or bowl	1802–1846	1	5	1	Floral pattern below border of semi-circles inside and out
Pearlware		Rim	Hollow form	1775–1840	1	5	1	
Whiteware	Handpainted—polychrome	Lid; body; base	Small covered dish	1820–1860	14	5	1	Hand-painted floral pattern; blue and green

Note: a. Maryland Archaeological Conservation Laboratory (2002).

throughout the eighteenth century. Early ware types such as Staffordshire-Type Slipped, Astbury, North Devon Gravel, and English brown stoneware were most common during the first half of the eighteenth century. Although tin-glazed wares were manufactured since the sixteenth century, this ware type remained in general use until the late eighteenth century. In the mid-eighteenth century this ware type was successively eclipsed first by white salt-glazed stoneware and later by creamware.

White salt-glazed stoneware was essentially a mid-eighteenth-century ware. Creamware and pearlware were the most common wares available during the late eighteenth century. However, by 1840, manufacture had stopped for both these ware types (circa 1820 for creamware and circa 1840 for some varieties of pearlware). The manufacturing dates for these common wares are primary indicators that some cultural behavior shift was happening by the mid-nineteenth century. Only four ware types represented at the Northern Burial Ground site (white ware, yellow ware, luster ware, and Guanajuato majolica) have nineteenth-century manufacturing dates; this is another indicator that there was a shift in cultural behavior within this black Nassau community sometime in the mid-nineteenth century (Wall 1994, 250–258; Noël-Hume 1991, 102–137; Miller, Martin, and Dickinson 1994, 238–244). This selection of table wares and tea wares, including Chinese export porcelain, is consistent with the types of ceramics available in eighteenth- and early-nineteenth-century British colonial markets.

Glass

Remains of at least five dark-green cylindrical wine bottles were excavated, as was one sherd of a four-sided case-type bottle. Apart from the shape, this last bottle did not include sufficient diagnostic detail to be analyzed more thoroughly. The details of a bottle's mouth and base are most diagnostic in determining the manufacturing technology used and therefore the general date range. Though reuse of bottles was common, bottles are still helpful for dating purposes; it is safe to assume that the deposition of a particular bottle type dates within twenty years of the documented manufacturing period for that type. Analysis of glass from this site was limited to these five bottles, the base and rim sherds of a leaded glass tumbler, the rim and body fragments of a delicate etched glass vessel, and a complete early-twentieth-century soft drink bottle.

Figure 6.17. Neck and mouth of an eighteenth-century wine bottle.

Bottle Mouth and Neck: circa 1761–1801

Research on this piece was based on the analysis of reliably dated examples by Parks Canada of English wine bottle glass dating from 1735 to 1850 (Figure 6.17). Beginning in the 1760s, the lip and the string rim of such bottles were tool-finished using a slightly different method than had been used up to that time. These finishing techniques did not change significantly until the early nineteenth century (Jones 1986, 33, 54–61). This piece was excavated from level 3 (40–60 centimeters) of Unit 5, just below the headstone.

Domed Bottle Base: Before Circa 1790

This example, from level 2 (20–40 centimeters) of the Test Unit, has the earlier high pushup base and exhibits the bulging heel (the turn from the body to the base) that is common on cylindrical bottles made before bottle-making technology changed in the 1820s (Jones 1986, 91–95). These features suggest that this bottle was made some time before 1790. It is not possible to refine this date estimation more without further diagnostic detail from the bottle.

Domed Bottle Base: Before Circa 1790

Sherds of this bottle base were recovered from level 2 of Unit 4. This base exhibits a bulging heel and distinct mark left by the pontil rod that would have held the bottle while the finish was created. The bulging heel suggests that this bottle was manufactured before the 1820s (Jones 1986, 91–95, 102–103).

Tool-Finished Mouth: Circa 1835 to 1855

Well-formed and even finishes such as in this example were created by adding glass for the finish. This type of finish generally dates after 1820. The variety that has a deliberate groove between the lip and the string rim has been dated to circa 1835 to 1855 based on archaeological examples (Figure 6.18). This style was made possible by the use of finish-forming tools (Jones 1986, 69–71). Although this example was also excavated from level 2 of Unit 4, it was not part of the same bottle as the bottle base that was described above.

Rickets-Molded Bottle: Circa 1820s

A mold line on a shoulder sherd identifies this as a sherd from a bottle made using a three-part Ricketts mold. This mold was patented in 1821 and was used in production from early 1822. It consisted of a cylindrical one-piece mold to form the body and two open-and-shut molds that formed the shoulder and neck. These parts left characteristic mold lines that encircled the body at the junction with the shoulder and two vertical lines that ex-

Figure 6.18. Tool-finished fragment of a bottle mouth.

tended from the shoulder junction up the neck (Jones 1986, 86–87, 90). The technology of Rickets-molded bottles meant that they had a straight, smooth transition from the heel to the base. This style of tooled finish dates to the 1820s and 1830s (ibid., 71, 91).

Leaded Glass Tumbler: Late Eighteenth to Early Nineteenth Centuries

Other eighteenth- or early nineteenth-century glass from this site included rim and base fragments of a leaded, colorless glass tumbler. The minimal amount of the body above the base suggests that it may have had a cylindrical shape. English lead glass tumblers of the eighteenth century were usually a conical shape, flaring outward slightly from the base to rim. In the early nineteenth century a straight-sided cylindrical form was also introduced. This feature suggests that this tumbler could date to the early nineteenth century. Tumblers were often undecorated and were manufactured in sizes ranging from half a gill to as much as a gallon, although half-pint and pint sizes were most common. They could be purchased in quantities of one, six, eight, or twelve. Into the nineteenth century manufacturers often let the pontil marks on tumblers unpolished, as is the case on the example we excavated at the Northern Burial Ground (Jones and Smith 1985, 35).

Acid-Etched and Enameled Drinking Glass: Nineteenth Century

This artifact was represented by two rim sherds and one body sherd of a delicate, non-leaded colorless glass container, possibly some type of drinking glass (Figure 6.19). The acid-etched and painted decorative techniques set these sherds apart from other glass we excavated. The amount of effort needed to complete this object suggests that it was relatively expensive. Designs etched in acid were achieved by first covering the object's surface with a compound such as wax. Next, a design was marked on the surface through the wax. A mix of hydrofluoric acid and ammonia would produce the frosted, obscured effect that is present on these sherds. This container was also decorated with enameled designs in several colors. Powdered colored glass that had a low melting temperature or was mixed with a flux was added to the glass surface. Since the compositions used in this process fused at different temperatures, it was necessary to fire the object several times, beginning with the color that fused at the highest temperature and ending with the color that fused at the lowest temperature (Jones and Sullivan et al. 1989, 55, 57).

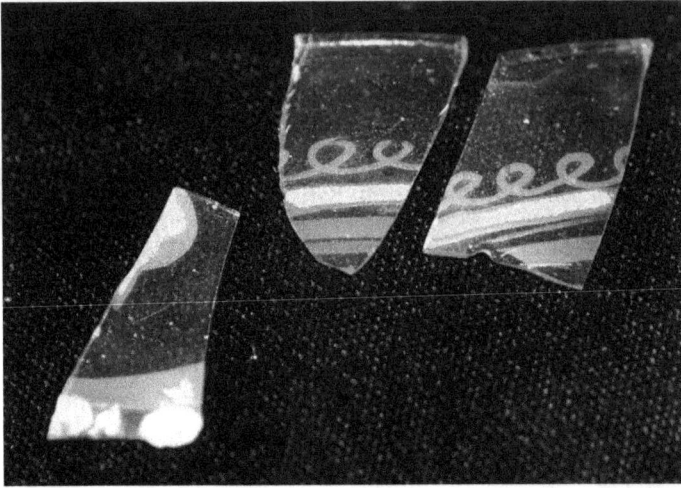

Figure 6.19. Acid-etched and painted drinking-glass sherds.

Soft-Drink Bottle: Early Twentieth Century

A complete amber-colored soft-drink bottle was excavated in level 2 of Unit 2. The bottle is machine-made with a crown top. It was likely not manufactured in the United States, as there has been no identification of any of the markings on the base. In view of the documentary and archaeological evidence for the use period of the cemetery site, I have assumed that this bottle was deposited at this site sometime after it was devastated by hurricanes in the 1920s and was possibly dropped at the time the original sidewalk was being constructed.

Faunal Remains

The most unexpected find from the excavation of a Test Unit was the evidence of butchered animal remains. Even factoring in the possibility that some of the faunal remains were casually deposited within the site by people passing through, it was important to explore a potential explanation for the amount and variety of butchered animal remains excavated (Table 6.3). For this reason, chicken, pork-chop, and fish bones were not collected because of the potential that these kinds of bones were all likely to have been deposited at the site after its use period as a cemetery. Chemical analysis would not be helpful in determining the general period when these food remains were deposited at the site. The most useful chronological indicators would be cultural markers such as evidence of butchering techniques and technology. Given the constraints of research time, the limited project funding, and the limited storage space at the lab, I decided not to keep machine-cut pork-chop bones, chicken bones, and fish bones. This was a controversial decision from an archaeological perspective, but given the constraints of this project I felt I could not follow all of the usual protocols.

Table 6.3. Catalog of faunal remains

Animal	Bone identity	How butchered	Unit	N	Comments
Horse/Donkey	Tooth		Test Unit	1	
Fish	Jaw		Unit 1	1	Species not identified
Fish	Vertebra		Unit 1	1	Smaller example; unidentified
Fish	Vertebra		Unit 2	1	Larger specimen; unidentified
Cattle	Rib	Handsawn	Unit 1	2	Very large animal; imported meat
Pig	Distal phalanx		Unit 1	1	
Pig	Proximal	Handsawn	Unit 2	1	
Pig	Axis vertebra	Handsawn		1	
Pig	Innominate (part of the pelvis)	Handsawn	Unit 4	2	
Pig	Deciduous tooth			1	
Unidentified	Small and eroded	Sawn (?)	Unit 2	1	
Rat	Femur		Unit 4	1	
Cattle	Vertebra	Chopped	Test Unit	1	
Cattle	Long bone	Chopped	Test Unit	1	
Pig or cattle	Rib	Handsawn		1	Handsawn and polished; evidence of long-term use
Turkey	Humerus	Sawn	Unit 1	1	Broadest end only partially sawn through
Large Pig/Cattle	Long bone		Unit 2	1	
Fish	Pectoral spines (?)		Unit 2	2	
Cattle	Tooth		Unit 5	1	

This type of material constitutes another category that has so far not been considered in the archaeology of African diaspora cemetery sites. A major factor contributing to this gap in archaeological knowledge is the way that African diaspora cemetery sites are often discovered and consequently excavated. Archaeologists do not often have opportunity to plan the excavation of unmarked cemetery sites, as these sites are usually uncovered only in the course of some development project. Archaeological investigation of this site provided an opportunity to understand the place of such animal remains within the site. Although the primary limitation for this research is the fact that the original site context had been disturbed, the cultural evidence that remained within the site can be assumed to have had some relation to the site's earlier cultural use.

I identified faunal remains in consultation with zooarchaeologists Joanne Bowen and Steve Archer at the Department of Archaeological Research at Colonial Williamsburg, Virginia. There was evidence of at least two butchering techniques. Most of the meat cuts had been sawn by hand. This method of butchering was common from the nineteenth century to the early twentieth century (Figure 6.20). One bone fragment appears to have been butchered using an implement such as a machete or a hatchet. The size of these large specimens suggested that the hand-sawn cuts of meat had been imported. Although some planters were raising cattle for local

Figure 6.20. Hand-sawn proximal phalanx of a pig.

consumption by the early 1800s, this was never a large-scale venture; most of the beef available locally was imported.

On his visit to Nassau in the early 1780s, German travel writer Johann Schoepf noted that "they take in from North America and from Europe fresh and salted meats, butter, rice, corn, wheat &c., utensils and clothing of every description" (1911, 272). The faunal remains at the Northern Burial Ground site are archaeological evidence of the urban black population's participation in this import economy.

Some locally produced meat was also available in Nassau. Charles Farquharson, a planter on San Salvador (or Watlings) Island, recounted in his journal a selection of livestock and crops that he shipped to market in Nassau: "Thursday. 24 Novr Four men at Sandy Point shiping the cows this morning the rest of the people weeding pastor. Shiped on board the Sloop altogether 6 head of Cattle 23 Sheep 9 Turkeys 2 Cups of Foules 18 Bushels of Guinea Corn" (1957, 45)

The faunal remains have been interpreted as archaeological evidence of food offerings left in the cemetery (Figure 6.21). I found no references in archaeological literature to evidence of food offerings in cemeteries. However, there are several such references in literature on folk culture, and this is the body of literature I have relied on. These include references in the work of Elsie Clews Parsons in 1918 on Andros Island in the Bahamas, the Georgia Writers' Project (1972), John McCarthy's 1997 work on Philadelphia's First Af-

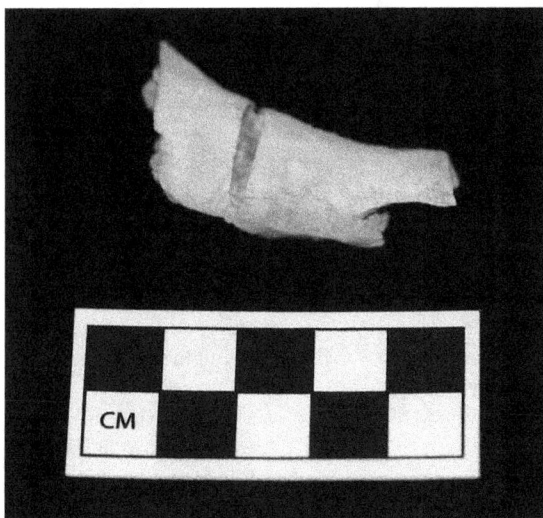

Figure 6.21. Butchering cut mark on a left turkey humerus.

rican Baptist Church cemeteries in the nineteenth century, and Grey Gundaker and Judith McWillie's 2005 publication on African American yard spaces.

I limited the retrieval of faunal remains because it was likely that most had been deposited long after the cemetery had been eviscerated. Paying close attention to butchering methods enabled us to collect only faunal bones that were not randomly deposited within this site and were evidence of some human activity related to the historic use of the site as a cemetery. This cultural activity combined with the practice of leaving personal items on graves supports the thesis that Bahamians of African descent maintained an African-derived cultural landscape within this cemetery during the eighteenth century and into the first half of the nineteenth century.

Other Cultural Material

Several other types of cultural material were excavated. These are artifacts that can be found in association with any western-style burials. However, one artifact did not fall in this category—a utensil handle that was likely put to a different cultural use than the European manufacturer intended (Table 6.4).

Table 6.4. Catalog of miscellaneous cultural materials

Artifact	Material	Manufactured	N	Unit	Comments
Disc	Copper	18th–19th centuries	3	Test Unit	Very thin, flat disc; unidentified
Stud fastener	Copper alloy	Late 19th century	1	Unit 1	
Spoon handle	Pewter (?)	19th century	1	Unit 1	Possibly originally placed as a utensil handle
Bahama penny	Copper alloy	20th century	1	Unit 1	Too eroded to decipher the date minted
Unidentified fragment	Plastic	20th century	1	Unit 1	
Slotted plate	Brass	20th century	1	Unit 1	Row of slots along one edge only
Lace pin	Gold	Late 19th century	1	Unit 2	Found in sandy matrix within cranium
Button—small	Shell	19th century	1	Unit 2	Machine-made outer ring and center ovoid
Round object	Bakelite (?)	19th century	1	Unit 2	Rim of small container with etched and painted designs

Artifact	Material	Manufactured	N	Unit	Comments
U.S. penny	Copper alloy	20th century	1	Unit 2	Too eroded to decipher the date minted
Crystalline stone	Pyrite	?	1	Unit 2	
Button—pressed metal	Copper alloy	Early 20th century	1	Unit 4	1902 design for U.S. General Services
Marble	Glass w color swirl	20th century	1	Unit 4	Chipped and broken
Metal fragment	Lead (?)	?	1	Unit 4	Possibly associated with nearby boating activity
Stone fragment	Slate	?	1	Unit 4	
Button—small	Shell	19th century	1	Unit 5	Four-hole sew-through; possibly from a child's clothing
Button—large	Shell	19th century	1	Unit 5	Decorated with ovoid shapes around edge + in center
Button	Glass/ Porcelain	19th century	1	Unit 5	Central copper alloy piece forming sew-through shank
Button	Plastic	20th century	1	Unit 5	Four-hole sew-through; possibly later-20th-century intrusion
Metal fragment	Lead (?)	?	1	Unit 5	Possibly associated with nearby boating activity
Nail	Iron	19th century	1	Unit 5	Corroded; appears to be round nail with a separated head
Headstone	Limestone	18th century	4	Unit 5	Locally made tablet stone reflects 18th-century head-stone styles
Liquor bottle covers	Aluminum	20th century	5	1, 2, 4	2 Bacardi, 1 Smirnoff, 1 BR&CO Ltd, 1 unidentified
Wood		?		TU, 1, 2	Samples of wood recovered but yet to be analyzed
Brick	Clay	18th–19th centuries		TU, 1, 4	Interpreted as likely a type of grave curbing material
Stone fragments		20th century		1, 2, 5	Interpreted as debris from sidewalk construction
Concrete	Cement + sand	20th century		1, 2, 4, 5	Interpreted as evidence of several sidewalks constructed
Nails, etc.	Iron	18th–20th centuries		All	No conservation facility in the Bahamas for small iron objects

Gold Lace Pin: Late Nineteenth Century

This was the only piece of personal jewelry we excavated. It was found in association with a cache of human skeletal remains that seemed to have been gathered for disposal off the site. Even though skeletal remains and cultural materials in this former cemetery site were gathered and discarded, I have assumed that this small gold pin was buried with the individual with whose partial remains it was excavated (Figure 6.22). This individual was likely an adult female. Late-nineteenth-century catalogues for Bloomingdale's (Bloomingdale Brothers 1988, 129–130), Montgomery Ward (Emmet 1969, 174–177), and Sears Roebuck (Israel 1968, 427–429) all list similar pieces of jewelry as a lace pin. Bar-shaped pins such as this example were available in an array of designs and materials, including solid gold (as is the case with this example), solid gold front, sterling silver, rolled gold, rolled plate, and gold-filled. Prices varied according to the quality of material; solid gold pins costed $1.25 and higher if precious stones were added. Rolled gold or gold-filled pins were the least expensive, at less than 50¢. This solid gold pin would have been relatively expensive.

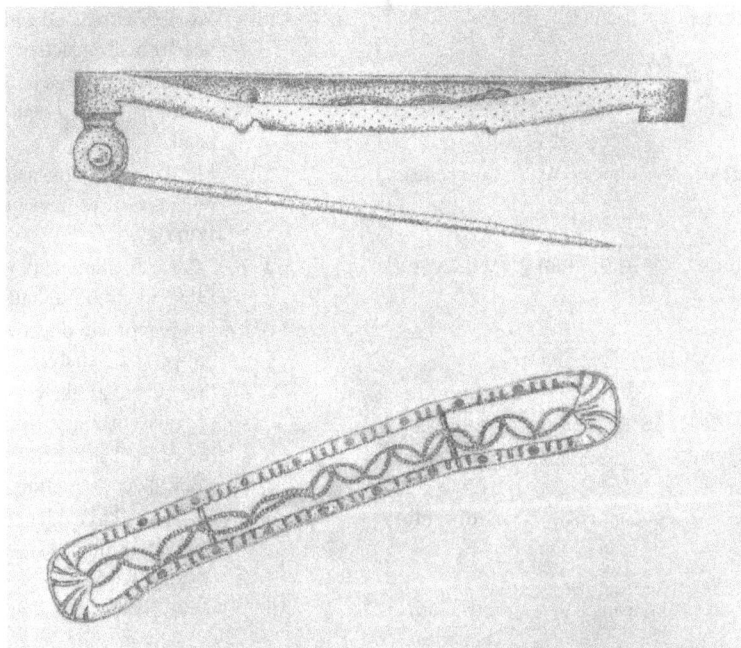

Figure 6.22. Drawing of the excavated gold filigree lace pin.

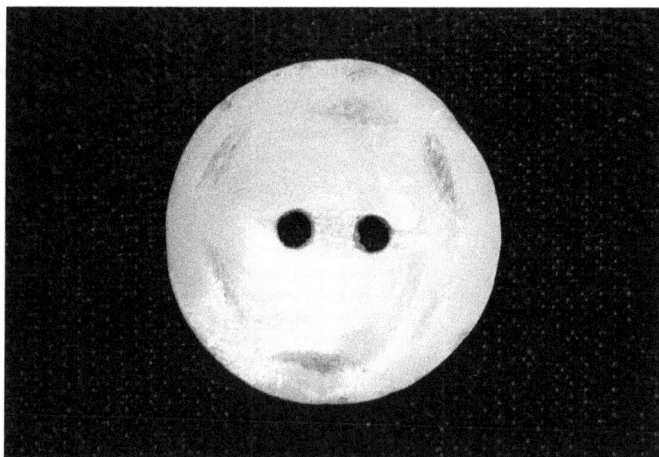

Figure 6.23. Shell button with incised decorative border.

Shell Buttons

The largest example of the three shell buttons that we found has an incised decorative border around the top face (Figure 6.23). Given this machine-produced design, I have dated this button to the mid-nineteenth century. Shell buttons are difficult to date definitively because shell has been used to make buttons for centuries. By the mid-nineteenth century, shell buttons were being mass produced in Europe and in the United States.

Metal Button

This button initially appeared to be an anomaly. Why a U.S. military–style button appeared in a British colony was unclear. The design motif on this flat, two-hole button made of a copper alloy consists of the iconic spread eagle below a disc encircled by stars (Figure 6.24). This two-hole form was made of thin metal pressed into the design template (Johnson 1948, 1:9, 67; 2: 24). Research revealed that this design, based on the Great Seal of the United States, was adopted in 1902 for the U.S. General Service (Wyckoff 1984, 92). Wyckoff noted that there was some latitude in allowing civilians to use regulation buttons as late as the 1930s (1984, 94).

Based on this information, I have interpreted this button as an artifact of the continuous migrations of African-descended Bahamians between the Bahamas and the United States since the 1870s. The individual who

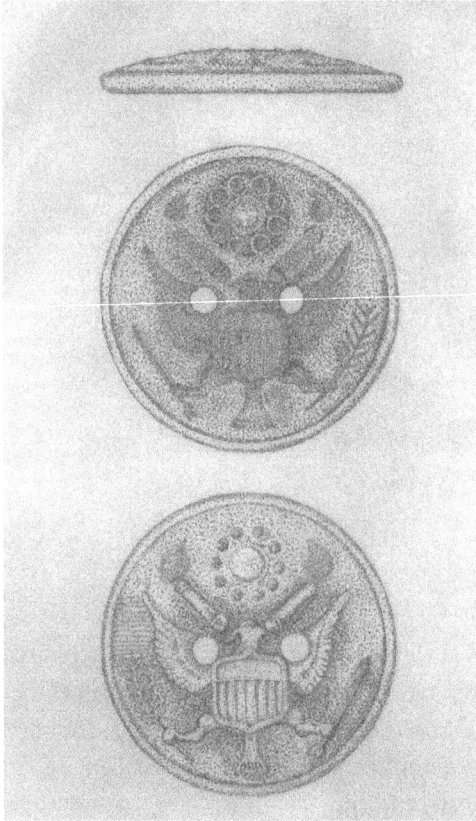

Figure 6.24. Drawing of a copper button with U.S. eagle crest.

was buried in clothing with this button had likely spent some time in the United States but was in the Bahamas when he died. The broad availability of official military material, such as this button, means that this Bahamian man did not have to be employed by the U.S. General Service. However, the 1902 adoption date for this specific button design suggests that this man was likely one of the last individuals to be buried within the Northern Burial Ground.

Leaded Utensil Handle

I have described this artifact as a leaded utensil handle because it is much heavier than its size would warrant. It appears that this artifact was deposited in its current form. I have not had it chemically analyzed, but, based on the amount of chemical change after being buried for some time, I have assumed that it was not manufactured in the first half of the twentieth cen-

Figure 6.25. Painted headstone carved from local limestone.

tury. Without further information about the original context of this artifact, I can only state that it had some cultural meaning that is lost to us now.

Limestone Headstone

This was the only headstone we uncovered during excavations at this site (Figure 6.25). It was made of limestone and was carved in a pattern that appears to be a local interpretation of contemporary eighteenth- and early nineteenth-century European or North American tablet stones. The stone is 70 centimeters long and 12 centimeters wide. There is no text on the stone, but the front panel is painted white with a black stripe across the rounded top. The outline of this stone resembles a human head and shoulders.

Lucayan Artifacts and Ecofacts

The indigenous inhabitants of the Bahamas are known as the Lucayan Taíno. They were the native people who met Christopher Columbus when he and his crew landed on an island in the archipelago that he renamed San Salvador but the Lucayans knew as Guanahaní. In less than fifty years after Columbus's voyage in 1492, the Lucayans were all gone from the Bahamas. The Spanish had taken them away as slaves.

The Spanish used Lucayans to work as pearl divers on Cubagua, a small island off the coast of Venezuela. Their swimming skills were highly valued in the pearl fisheries, where it was necessary to dive to great depths. However, this work was even more physically demanding than working in the gold mines. Slaving raids continued until at least 1520, when an expedition failed to find any potential slaves until they reached the coast of Florida (Las Casas [1527–1562] 1965, 3:501–502).

Current archaeological knowledge states that Lucayans began migrating into the Bahamian archipelago (which includes the Turks and Caicos Islands) from both Hispaniola and Cuba about AD 660 to 865. In the Lucayos (the name by which Lucayans and other Taíno referred to these islands), the Lucayans relied heavily on marine resources such as fish, sea turtles, and monk seals. But they also hunted land animals such as iguana, birds, and other small mammals. They cultivated cassava as their staple root crop (Keegan 1997, 27; Rouse 1992, 100–101).

Lucayans built their settlements on the lee side of coastal dunes, usually on the lee coast of islands. This strategy gave them easy access to the ocean and access to fresh water and inland resources. Settlers who came after the Lucayans also preferred to live near the coast, for the same reasons the Lucayans did. This means that for later archaeological periods, evidence of earlier Lucayan occupation is likely to be encountered quite often. As historical archaeological research continues throughout the Bahamas, multi-component coastal sites should be expected. Because European and African peoples used this property continuously for at least 200 of the 300 years Nassau was settled, the Lucayan component of this site is fragmentary at best (Table 6.5). The following artifacts are documented as evidence of the earlier Lucayan site.

Palmetto Ware

This term refers to locally made Lucayan ceramics. Palmetto ware was the predominant type of several Lucayan ceramic styles. Bahama red loam clay soil was used to form the paste for this ceramic. The paste color is red to orange-brown, usually with a darker-colored core. Palmetto ware has limestone inclusions and a temper of crushed, burned shell (Figure 6.26). Vessels are primarily round and boat-shaped bowls 20–40 centimeters in diameter and 5–20 centimeters high. Palmetto ware griddles were flat and about 30–60 centimeters in diameter.

Table 6.5. Catalog of Lucayan cultural materials, shells, and coral

Artifact/Ecofact	Material	Unit	N	Comments
Ceramic	Clay and temper	Test Unit	4	Palmetto ware-type ceramic
Utensil	Conch shell	Test Unit	1	*Strombus gigas*; 3 notches on 1 edge of inner whorl
Ceremonial tool	Igneous rock	Unit 4	1	Broken; top half recovered
Possible palm frond	Plant	Unit 4	1	Burned fragment; plant species not identified
Ceremonial tool	Olivine basalt	Unit 5	1	Only a flake recovered
Food shell	Codakia	Test Unit	1	*Codakia obicularis*
Food shell	Whelk	Test Unit	2	*Livona pica*
Food shell	Conch shell	Test Unit	2	*Strombus gigas*
Misc. shells	Conch and crab	Test Unit	4	*Strombus gigas* and *Strombus alatus*; includes juveniles
Food shell	Codakia	Unit 2	5	*Codakia obicularis*
Food shell	Conch shell	Unit 2	12	*Strombus gigas*
Food shell	Whelk	Unit 2	3	*Livona pica*
Food shell	Ladder shell	Unit 2	1	*Cerithidea scalariformis*
Seashell (not used for food)	Moon shell	Unit 2	1	*Polinices lactea*; possibly deposited in storm surge; cut in half, possibly Lucayan
Seashell	Striate Tellin	Unit 2	4	*Merisca aequistriata*
Seashell	Various conch species	Unit 2	3	*Strombus gigas* and *Strombus alatus*; juveniles
Seashell	Alternate Tellin	Unit 2	1	*Tellina alternata*
Seashell	Blood ark	Unit 2	1	*Lunarca ovalis*
Seashell	Elegant Dosinia	Unit 2	3	*Dosinia elegans*
Echinoderm	Sea biscuit	Unit 2	2	*Eurhodia rugosa*
Coral	Elkhorn	Unit 2	1	*Acropora palmata*; likely deposited in storm surge
Coral	Staghorn	Unit 2	1	*Acropora cervicornis*; cultural use by Lucayans
Food shell	Chiton	Unit 5	1	Just 1 plate recovered
Food shell	Whelk	Unit 5	1	*Livona pica*; small but complete

Figure 6.26. Lucayan Palmetto ware sherd.

Figure 6.27. A Lucayan notched conch-shell implement.

Conch Shell Implement

The Lucayan diet and lifestyle relied substantially on marine resources such as conch (*Strombus gigas*). The shell of this large marine mollusk provided the most common local material sufficiently durable to be used for tools. This fragment of the inner whorl of a conch shell stood out as a deliberately manipulated artifact because of the three notches that were made in one of the long straight edges (Figure 6.27). It is unclear what the function of

Figure 6.28. Fragment of a Lucayan ceremonial stone tool.

this implement was, but it adds to our insight into the level of creativity of Lucayans as they constructed the resources to meet their daily needs.

Ceremonial Tool Fragments

Figure 6.28 shows half of a ceremonial stone tool. This type of artifact is thought to have had some ceremonial or symbolic purpose because the entire surface is highly polished and there are no signs of wear on the edges that would indicate use. Lucayans valued these objects highly; they are often found in burial contexts. They stand out in Bahamian sites because these were all made of nonlocal stone. This is evidence that Lucayans may have acquired these prized cultural objects through trade. The example in Figure 6.28 is made of a type of basalt. Stephen Clement, a professor of geology at the College of William and Mary, has identified a second flake from a larger implement, also excavated at the Northern Burial Ground site, as olivine basalt. With further research, it might be possible to determine more specifically where these stones were imported from.

7

Conclusion

My goal in this project was to assess to what extent an African-influenced cemetery landscape was visible through time in the archaeological record. I considered four landscape features and assessed the physical impact of daily life on the bodies of members of this community. I considered the site's location near water and assessed whether this was likely a deliberate factor in situating the cemetery. I also assessed whether trees were used as memorial grave markers. Archaeological investigation of the site enabled me to assess two other cultural practices that were part of the African-derived culturally constructed landscape of this cemetery space: placing personal items on top of graves and putting out food offerings for the spirits of loved ones. These cultural practices were an integral part of the culturally constructed landscape that was created within this space and was maintained for the almost 200 years this space was used as a cemetery.

A primary limitation of my research was the fact that much of the original archaeological context for this site has been destroyed. This meant that I could not record specific details about the treatment of individual burials within the site. It also meant that I could make only limited assessments about any skeletal remains that were recovered. The information I do have about the human skeletal remains that were excavated is of limited use because the samples are too small to be representative of this particular cemetery population or of the larger community this burial ground served. Any skeletal and dental pathologies I noted could only be cited as individual examples that have the potential to help us formulate questions about what kinds of challenges communities such as this one faced with regard to health and sanitation.

A key component of this project is situating any research on human remains within a larger context to understand how the lives of the community intersected with the cultural landscape they created within this cemetery over time. Although the original cemetery context of this site has been destroyed, archaeological research proceeded on the assumption that any remaining cultural material within the site that predates the devastation of the hurricanes of the 1920s can be assumed to be related to the site's period of use as a cemetery.

My analysis of the ceramics we excavated suggested that the use period for the cemetery predates the late-eighteenth-century date suggested in documentary records. This finding gives new insight into the siting of the Northern Burial Ground across the street from Centre Burial Ground, which is known to be an early-eighteenth-century cemetery because of dates on the earliest grave markers. The artifacts we recovered indicate that the Northern Burial Ground was contemporary with Centre Burial Ground. This opens a new hypothesis for how the cemetery was established. Instead of simply being relegated to a marginal location, this perspective touts the cultural agency of Africans in the Atlantic diaspora. This property was not recognized as prime real estate by the dominant society because it was on the edge of Nassau's economic hub which was centered on Nassau's harbor. Adding to the cemetery's convenience for a segment of Nassau's urban black community was its location adjacent to a white cemetery. The siting of the black cemetery opposite the white cemetery likely had to be approved by local Anglican officials because the Anglican Church managed and maintained all public cemeteries in the colony from the late seventeenth century. The process of obtaining legal title to property in the Bahamas remained unsettled until 1783, when Loyalist immigrants to the Bahamas needed grants of land so they could cultivate plantations.[1] In 1768, Governor Shirley cited the inability to grant legal title to land as a serious impediment to the economic development of the colony.[2] Blacks were able to use this uncertain legal environment to their advantage and make use of land.[3]

Before the arrival of Loyalist immigrants to the Bahamas in the 1780s, there was no social or legal requirement that blacks be buried in separate cemetery spaces. Until about 1790, existing Christ Church records, which date to the first half of the eighteenth century, recorded baptisms, marriages and burials as they happened and noted the color and status of free blacks and slaves. By 1790, after Loyalist immigrants were fully settled in

Nassau, the records for nonwhites were recorded in the back pages of these registers.[4] St. Matthew's Parish was created in 1795 as the second parish for New Providence. All of its registers were recorded using this racially segregated format.[5] The written records reflected how physical spaces were treated. I have assumed that if a separate cemetery space was established in the first half of the eighteenth century, the black community chose to have a cemetery space exclusively for their use to enable them to observe and maintain African-derived cultural practices. A separate cemetery space enabled this community to make a public presentation of their cultural identity. Anyone, white or black, living in the Bahamas (and visitors who were familiar with other African Diaspora communities in the Americas) would have understood what community was represented in that cemetery.

Although this site was not in the center of the town, it was in a highly visible location on the only road to the eastern end of the island. Recognizing the agency of African-descended people in situating the Northern Burial Ground is only half of the equation. The dominant society, which was shaped by the class-based British model, tolerated this different cultural landscape. Bahamians of European descent were aware of the fact that the black community memorialized its dead quite differently than they did. Evidently as long as Africans and African-descended people did so in spaces that were not significant in the wider society, they were allowed to memorialize their dead as they saw fit. J. W. Orderson described slave memorials for the dead he had observed at the Fontabelle slave cemetery on the western edge of Bridgetown, Barbados, in about 1776 (Orderson [1842] 2002, 43).

Perhaps the willingness of the British colonists to allow blacks to observe non-British burial customs can be attributed, in part, to the fact that until the second half of the eighteenth century, British cemeteries functioned as multipurpose sites. Earlier British public cemeteries were often spaces where events such as markets and fairs were held. I have supposed that since British people were familiar with the use of cemetery spaces for events other than burials, they would have been more amenable to allowing Africans to memorialize burials in the ways they preferred. Because colonial society in the British Caribbean was based on British culture and society, any cultural change in Britain would be reflected in British West Indian colonies. In the late eighteenth century, the British began treating cemetery spaces as serene, park-like spaces with pathways and trees that provided shade. This change may have influenced British attitudes toward African-derived burial practices. For example, in their excavation of New Seville plantation on Jamaica's northwest coast, Douglas Armstrong and Mark Fleischman (2003) discovered several burials in house yards in the area of an early slave village that dated from the seventeenth to the late eighteenth centuries. However, they found no burials in house yards in the area of a later slave village that dated from the late eighteenth to the late nineteenth centuries. This change suggests that by the late eighteenth century laborers in this enslaved community were allowed to bury their dead only in the churchyard cemetery.

From this perspective, the late-eighteenth-century documentation was meant to formalize control of this cemetery site that already existed, particularly in light of policies by recent Loyalist migrants that emphasized the racial segregation of all public spaces. St. Matthew's Anglican Church administered and physically maintained the Northern Burial Ground, apparently until it was closed in the first decade of the twentieth century. In the late nineteenth century, the Board of Works erected a wall around the Northern Burial Ground that was topped by a wooden picket fence. The fact that no similar wall was built around Centre Burial Ground suggests that the wall was a means of screening the most controversial elements of this non-western-style cemetery landscape from public view. The different means of enclosure for the two cemetery spaces (the records note only that Centre Burial Ground was enclosed by a fence) could indicate a less tolerant attitude by nineteenth-century Anglican Church officials toward the continued practice of African-derived burial customs within this cemetery.[6]

The use pattern of the artifacts we recovered fits with the African-derived cultural action of placing personal items on top of graves, particularly eating utensils. It appears that this cultural behavior changed quite rapidly sometime in the mid-nineteenth century. The most likely change that affected Nassau's black residents was the process of emancipation. Although the Emancipation Act went into effect on August 1, 1834, full emancipation was not granted to former slaves until 1838. I propose that this change in cultural behavior reflected a new reality Bahamian blacks faced in a free society. With the elimination of the legal and social restrictions of enslavement, blacks could choose to move beyond the bounds of a slaveholding society. In an urban environment, former slaves had access to greater social and economic opportunities. After full emancipation, former slaves were free to live and work where they chose, although wage-earning opportunities were limited for former slaves in the Bahamas for the rest of the nineteenth century. Because most wages were paid in kind and employers often extended credit to their laborers, most blacks and their descendants in the Bahamas became enmeshed in a system of truck and credit. The Truck Act of 1907 brought an end to these nefarious practices by legislating that workers in Eleuthera's pineapple industry and masters and seamen on sponging and turtling vessels were to be paid their wages in cash.[7] Despite these challenges, the principles of choice and freedom are powerful concepts for any humans. The changes the black community of Nassau made in how they memorialized their dead may have been deemed necessary because the dominant society did not value African-derived cultural behavior.

The example of Monday Ranger illustrates this point. He was buried in Potter's Field, the public cemetery on the western side of Nassau that was originally intended for the burial of whites, particularly those who were not Anglican. This was one of the cemeteries the new bishop of Jamaica dedicated in 1826. Bethlehem, the western cemetery intended for blacks, is located about a quarter mile south of Potter's Field, atop a hill at the northern edge of the "Over-the-Hill" area that was a free black community since at least the second half of the eighteenth century. However, since 1833, even before emancipation, Gov. Balfour had instructed Anglican clergy to stop separating burials in public cemeteries by race. By 1902, when he died, Monday Ranger's family could choose to have him buried in Potter's Field, the higher-status former white cemetery, instead of in the Bethlehem cemetery.

Such facts as his birthplace in Lagos, Nigeria, and his name of Monday (the anglicized form of his West African day name) suggest that he was a liberated African[8] who had been freed from a slave ship intercepted by the Royal Navy and resettled in Nassau. After the British Parliament abolished the slave trade in 1807, the first African captives were landed in the Bahamas in 1811.[9] These African captives, also referred to as liberated Africans, were treated as apprentices. Those who arrived before 1825 were apprenticed to planters, usually in Nassau, typically for a period of seven years.[10] Liberated African men were also the main source of recruits for the black troops of the West India Regiments. The legal status of liberated Africans as free people of color enabled them to achieve social and economic statuses that were generally unattainable for individuals who had experienced slavery in the Bahamas, even after they were freed.

There is evidence that liberated Africans relied on this critical difference in status to distinguish themselves from enslaved individuals (Buckley 1979). Nevertheless, in the wider society, liberated Africans were still seen as Africans. It was in their interest to minimize any perceptions of themselves as culturally African and therefore "uncivilized" so they could make the most of the potential privileges their status allowed them. There was immense pressure from whites for liberated Africans to become Europeanized. As Roseanne Adderley explains it, "Far more so than slaves, liberated Africans had the opportunity to consider and engage their status and identity as migrants. Nonetheless, during the nineteenth century, British opinion continued to view African cultures as at best inferior and more often as savage or barbaric. Therefore, although liberated Africans entered the Caribbean as free people, they too faced a European society bent on de-Africanizing them. Indeed, the project of settling liberated Africans in the West Indies had always included the civilization, or cultural "improvement" of Africans as one of their aims" (Adderley 2006, 208).

Although Monday Ranger was born in Africa, he evidently chose to adopt a public identity that was more valued in a society where an acceptance of British social and economic values was the cultural basis for being seen as a member of a social class that was higher than the class status of the masses of working poor. He had been so successful in making this cultural transition that even in death his family had him interred in the still predominantly white Potter's Field cemetery. Although it was likely not imperative that socially successful liberated Africans such as Monday Ranger become members of the Anglican Church, they would have been expected to show a command of the king's (or queen's) English and a familiarity with the nuances of British social behavior.

I argue that the black community that used the Northern Burial Ground made this cultural transition only when it became socially expedient to do so. Less public aspects of an African-derived cultural heritage remained part of their cultural repertoire for more than a century after emancipation. Such cultural carryovers included a language variant that blended English words with West African structural elements (such as grammar and sentence construction) and the custom of burying a baby's umbilical cord (a cultural practice that I know from personal experience continued at least until the 1970s) as a means of establishing a sense of place and belonging.

Despite the removal of burials and related grave materials in the 1930s, my archaeological investigations recovered a wide array of cultural material that I have interpreted as remnants of personal items left on top of graves. The fact that sherds of early eighteenth-century ceramics and glass remained within the cemetery site suggests that the practices St. Matthew's Church used to maintain this property generally left the objects community members had placed on graves in place. Instead, church officials constructed a low wall to partially conceal these African-derived cultural practices.

Based on my analysis of the ceramic types we excavated, a probable period for the establishment of the Northern Burial Ground is the 1720s or 1730s, after Nassau's turbulent period as a haven for pirates had ended. The earliest dated grave marker in Centre Burial Ground supports this thesis. My analysis of glass sherds revealed that the earliest examples date to the mid-eighteenth century. One possible explanation for the difference in the earliest dates for these two artifact types may be that earlier drinking vessels were made of some type of locally available gourd, stoneware, or a refined redware. The suggestion here is that this urban black community expressed their cultural agency by exhibiting and maintaining African-derived means of memorializing their dead. This African-influenced cultural behavior would have served to reinforce the identity of community members and their sense of belonging.

This community had access to a wide array of tablewares, tea wares, storage vessels, utilitarian vessels, and specialty items made of ceramic and glass. Although the Bahamas was a small, relatively poor colony, Nassau's harbor provided a link to regional and global commercial networks. Urban black communities participated in these networks to whatever extent they were financially able to do so.

The most dramatic finding of the artifact analysis was the ending manufacture dates for ceramics and glass. For both categories, the periods of availability are predominantly through much of the eighteenth century and into the first third of the nineteenth century. We recovered only a few glass and ceramic sherds that date to the second half of the nineteenth century (5 percent of the ceramic types identified), even though the cemetery remained in use until the early twentieth century. The glass and ceramic evidence strongly suggests that the African-Bahamian community that used the Northern Burial Ground practiced African-derived customs of memorialization from the early eighteenth century to the mid-nineteenth century. Even the arrival of Loyalists, who were highly intolerant of African cultural practices, had not stamped out these customs. So what explains the abrupt shift in frequency of these customs in the 1840s?

The most likely explanation was the advent of full emancipation within the British Empire after 1838. As had been the case with liberated Africans before that date, the elimination of legal bondage afforded formerly enslaved laborers broader opportunities, at least in theory. But those opportunities came at a cultural price. After 1838, the Anglican Church opened chapels in black communities just outside Nassau and established free schools for black children on New Providence and throughout the Bahamas. That is when workers who had been slaves in the Bahamas had the first opportunity to make choices about integrating with white society.

For blacks who wanted to be socially mobile, what they conveyed to later generations was that people who were educated and culturally adept certainly did not engage in such cultural activities as placing personal dishes on top of a grave or leaving food offerings for spirits. Even though these representations of an African-derived cultural heritage likely reinforced cultural identity and provided a sense of reassurance, they seem to have faded quickly. However, I suggest that less visible aspects of an African-derived cultural identity, such as burying a baby's umbilical cord (McNeil 1998, 18; Greene 2002, 67–68), were maintained for more than a century longer, continuing into the last third of the twentieth century.

I use the example of my umbilicus to illustrate how such an overtly African-derived cultural behavior was maintained by generations of African-Bahamians who were also faithful adherents of the Anglican Church. My mother, whose maternal family has been Anglican at least since the mid-nineteenth century, told me that she buried my umbilical cord at the foot of one of the row of tall casuarina trees (*Casuarina equisetifolia*) lining the bay road in Governor's Harbour, Eleuthera (Figure 7.1). She explained that this meant that I was as much a part of that place as it had become a part of me. When a Bahamian of African descent declares "My nabel string bury dere," it is an assertion that s/he has an inalienable right to belong to that place. In the Bahamas, the umbilicus is generally buried at the foot of a large tree. Details of this action are a very private aspect of an African-derived cultural heritage and are usually only known by the individual whose umbilicus has been buried and his/her most intimate relatives.

This examination of African-derived memorialization practices illustrates

Figure 7.1. Casuarina trees, Governor's Harbour, Eleuthera.

and documents one of the many processes of creolization. For people of African descent, this process was continually being negotiated and changes in cultural behavior were conceded only as life circumstances required. This is not a short-term, finite historical process, as is sometimes implied. For people of African descent, more than for those of European heritage, there was a continuous need to engage in some level of cultural shifting in order to maneuver through the demands of a wider Eurocentric society. I chose to use Du Bois's concept of "double consciousness" rather than the broader term "creolization" because I felt that the concept of double consciousness more aptly conveys the fact that people of African descent often make cultural decisions, consciously or unconsciously, that mediate between the need to participate in a broader society and the desire to maintain an African-derived cultural sense of being and belonging. The process of creating a double consciousness is an aspect of the process of creolization. My aim was to examine this process from the perspective of an African-descended population and to detail how such a community was able to negotiate some of the processes of cultural change.

Africans in the Americas were required to bury their dead in Christian or European-style cemeteries, and they often also observed other European-derived burial practices such as burial in a coffin with the body oriented east to west and facing east. For populations in urban areas, where Africans could exercise greater autonomy, these basic burial practices could be combined with African-derived burial practices such as locating cemeteries near a body of water, using large trees as "sacred groves" for individual graves or using a single tree to serve an entire cemetery, placing personal items on top of graves, and leaving food as an offering to ancestral spirits. A significant contribution from this research is my hypothesis of the possible circumstances that led to the discontinuation of these very public displays of African-derived cultural activity.

Although the British were the first European colonial power to outlaw the slave trade and the institution of slavery, the evidence of what African-Bahamians faced in the post-emancipation years demonstrates the extent to which cultural affiliation was a product of the larger social order. In the post-emancipation years in the Bahamas, the Anglican Church became the state-approved social and cultural guardian that sought to impart "civilizing" British/European ways to former slaves and free people of color. From the late 1830s to the 1840s, the Anglican Church established chapels and free elementary schools throughout the Bahamas. Several served black communities on New Providence Island, where Nassau is located. The unspoken message conveyed was that these institutions provided the models for how to be good colonial subjects. Neither of these models, however, included any economic pathways to help with this transition.

In the 1880s, Louis D. Powles, a colonial official, noted the pervasive system of economic bondage in which most black Bahamians found themselves. Without the right social and financial connections, access to minimal education and adherence to the Anglican religion did little to give African-Bahamians a route to higher social status. Most black Bahamians were excluded from upward mobility. From the mid-nineteenth century, the African-Bahamians who used the Northern Burial Ground expressed double consciousness. They conducted their public selves as good Anglicans and civilized British subjects in the hope of improving their access to a better living. But to draw upon a stabilizing sense of identity and a sense of belonging, they could choose to rely privately on the reassurance of an African-derived cultural heritage.

NOTES

Introduction: Basic Assumptions

1. This was the full name for this cemetery until 1833, when Gov. Balfour instructed Anglican clergy to stop categorizing cemeteries in racial terms. "The Humble Petition of William Hepworth—officiating minister and Andrew Seton and Dugald Blair Church Wardens and the undersigned Magistrates and Inhabitants of the Parish of Saint Matthew in the Island of New Providence one of the said Bahama Islands on behalf of themselves and the rest of the Inhabitants of the said Parish," May 16, 1826, Anglican Church Diocese Records, Jamaica Archives, Spanish Town, Gov. Balfour to July 7, 1833, folios 235–236, Colonial Office CO23/88, Department of Archives, Nassau.

Chapter 1. An Overview of Bahamian History in Context

1. "A List of the Names of the People which gave Security in the feere voyages and office after their arrivall here in the ship fancy, 1699," Colonial Office Correspondence CO5 1257/B16, Department of Archives, Nassau.

2. *Bahama Gazette*, December 11–18, 1784, 1, and October 1–8, 1785, 2–3, Department of Archives, Nassau.

3. Gov. Montfort Browne, New Providence, to the Earl of Dartmouth, Secretary of State for the Colonies, London, May 6, 1775, folios 28–33, Colonial Office CO23/23, Department of Archives, Nassau.

4. Gov. Thomas Shirley, Nassau, to the Earl of Hillsborough, Secretary of State for the Colonies, December 9, 1768, folio 7, Colonial Office CO23/8, Department of Archives, Nassau.

5. Ibid, folio 3.

6. Gov. Browne to the Earl of Dartmouth, May 6, 1775. The transfer of title to land in the Bahamas from the lord proprietors back to the British Crown was not executed until 1783, when Loyalist immigrants began arriving in the Bahamas from the former American colonies. General Index, 1700–1850, Book N, 229–259, Registrar General's Department, Nassau.

7. Instructions from Lieutenant Colonel Robert Morse, Chief Engineer, New York,

July 14, 1783, Fort Charlotte Research Collection, Antiquities, Monuments & Museum Corporation, Nassau.

8. Gov. Thomas Shirley, Nassau, December 9, 1768, to the Earl of Hillsborough, Secretary of State for the Colonies, folio 8, Colonial Office CO23/8, Department of Archives, Nassau.

9. Until the mid- to late nineteenth century, a distinction was routinely made between blacks (those with predominantly African physical features) and people of color (those of mixed racial ancestry). Here, however, these terms are used interchangeably, because when referring to groups that included a variety of individuals it was usual to use the term "people of colour."

10. Instructions from Lieutenant Colonel Morse, July 14, 1783.

11. *The Bahama Gazette*; Register of Freed Slaves, Department of Archives, Nassau.

12. Ministry of Works Board of Works Minute Books, 1863–1923, volume 1914–1915, 24, Department of Archives, Nassau; 1788 map of the town of Nassau, Department of Archives, Nassau.

13. Wylly (1789); Gov. Dunmore, Most Secret and Confidential Despatch to Lord Grenville, Secretary of State for the Colonies, London, 1787, folio 149, Colonial Office CO23/28. Department of Archives, Nassau.

14. Instructions from Lieutenant Colonel Morse, July 14, 1783.

15. Gov. Browne to the Earl of Dartmouth, May 6, 1775.

16. Husbands, regardless of race, could assume control of the material and financial property of their wives. That these men were not white was significant because of their access to greater material wealth.

17. Advertisements in *The Bahama Gazette*, 1786–1800, Department of Archives, Nassau.

18. Dunmore, Most Secret and Confidential Despatch.

19. "Out Islands" was the term used to refer to islands in the Bahamas other than New Providence, where the capital of Nassau is located. Culturally this term reinforced a sense of separation and isolation from Nassau, the center of political and economic activity for the country. After the Bahamas attained political independence in 1973, the name for these other islands was changed to "Family Islands," which conveys a sense of inclusion rather than exclusion.

20. Queries on the Culture of Cotton, May 16, 1800, folios 166–210, Colonial Office CO23/39, Department of Archives, Nassau.

21. Morgan (1999, 26–27); Gov. Dunmore to Lord Grenville, Secretary of State for the Colonies, London, March 14, 1791, folios 232–233, Colonial Office CO23/30; Gov. Dowdeswell to Lord Grenville, May 25, 1799, folio 201, Colonial Office CO23/38. Both in Department of Archives, Nassau.

22. Buckley (1979, 20–21); Robert Hunt, president of the Legislative Council, Nassau, to Duke of Portland, Secretary of State for the Colonies, London, May 9, 1801, folios 132–133, Colonial Office CO23/39, Department of Archives, Nassau.

23. Robert Hunt to Duke of Portland, May 9, 1801.

24. Vice Admiralty Court Minutes, September 29, 1809, Department of Archives, Nas-

sau. The Vice Admiralty Court decided on the disposition of vessels that were brought in by Bahamian wreckers or acquired as prizes of war. Decisions were also made regarding the disposition of goods from vessels, including slaves.

25. Vice Admiralty Court Minutes, October 31, 1809, Department of Archives, Nassau.

26. Africans rescued from slave ships by the Royal Navy were referred to by several terms, including liberated Africans, new negroes, and recaptives. Once they had been condemned to the Crown they were generally known as apprentices. During the period 1834 to 1838, when former slaves were required to serve an apprenticeship period, they were also known as African apprentices. Report of Stipendiary Magistrate Thomas Winder to Gov. Cockburn, 1835, folios 367–382, Colonial Office CO23/93, Department of Archives, Nassau.

27. William Vesey Munnings to the Lord Viscount Castlereagh, February 19, 1810, folios 9–11, Colonial Office CO23/57, Department of Archives, Nassau.

28. Munnings to Castlereagh, February 19, 1810, folios 12–15, Colonial Office CO23/57, Department of Archives, Nassau.

29. Earl of Liverpool to Mr. Munnings, October 30, 1811, folios 63–64, Colonial Office CO23/58, Department of Archives, Nassau. "47 Geo.3.C.36" refers to the Slave Trade Abolition Act of 1807.

30. Case No.12, Vice Admiralty Court proceedings, Mr. Munnings to the Earl of Liverpool, October 6, 1811, folios 42–48, Colonial Office CO23/58, Department of Archives, Nassau.

31. Gov. Grant, Nassau, to Earl of Bathurst, Secretary of State for the Colonies, London, November 9, 1824, folio 1053, Governors' Despatches, 1818–1825, Department of Archives, Nassau.

32. Gov. B. T. Balfour, Nassau, to G. G. Stanley, June 7, 1833, Governors' Despatches, folios 234–236, Colonial Office CO23/88, Department of Archives, Nassau.

33. Edwin Stephen, born August 19, 1818, son of Phebe Sergeant and Stephen Dillett; Cecelia Emily Lenora, born January 31, 1821, daughter of Phebe Sergeant and Stephen Dillette; Thomas William Henry, born September 29, 1823, son of Stephen and Charlotte Dillette; Joseph Eugene, born March 9, 1826, son of Stephen and Charlotte Dillette; Catharine Augusta, born July 31, 1828, daughter of Stephen and Charlotte Dillet; all in Christ Church Births and Baptisms Register, "Coloured," 1805–1828, Department of Archives, Nassau.

34. Votes of the House of the Assembly 1828–1831, 17–18, 30–33, 83, and 95, Department of Archives, Nassau.

35. Votes of the House of Assembly, December 22, 1829, 81, Department of Archives, Nassau

36. Gov. Cockburn to Lord Stanley, Secretary of State for the Colonies, November 17, 1841, CO23/110/307–327, Department of Archives, Nassau; Confidential despatch from Lord Stanley to Gov. Cockburn enclosing a copy of the report by law officers for the Crown, January 31, 1842, CO23/110/330–333, Department of Archives, Nassau.

37. Gov. Grant, Nassau, to Lord Bathurst, Secretary of State for the Colonies, Governors' Despatches, 1824, folios 1019–1024. Department of Archives, Nassau.

Chapter 2. African Influence on Eighteenth- and Nineteenth-Century Cemeteries

1. Some information is found in the Christ Church vestry minutes about the weeding, cleaning, and upkeep of this cemetery; Minutes of Christ Church Vestry, 1870–1910, Records of the Anglican Church, Department of Archives, Nassau. Government records have some information on the construction and repair of walls enclosing public cemeteries such as Bethlehem; Ministry of Works Index, P. W. D. Minutes, Specs, Contracts, etc. 1863–1923, Department of Archives, Nassau.

Chapter 3. European Influence on Eighteenth- and Nineteenth-Century Cemeteries

1. "I have thought proper to lay before you and to recommend to your consideration a Copy of a Letter which I have received from His Majesty's Secretary of State respecting the making due provision for the Establishment of Churches and Ministers in such of these Islands as shall appear most Expedient and requisite." Gov. Dunmore to the House of Assembly, July 10, 1792, Votes of the House of Assembly, 1792, 10–11, Department of Archives, Nassau.

2. In 1852, Gov. John Gregory, who was Roman Catholic, died during his term in office in the Bahamas and was buried in Potter's Field (McDermott 1960, 27).

3. "Mr. Forbes with leave brought in a Bill entitled 'An Act for defraying the Expence of enclosing the Church yard (Christ Church) and Burying Grounds in and about the Town of Nassau.'" May 1, 1789, Votes of the House of Assembly, 1789, 134–136, Department of Archives, Nassau.

4. "An Act of Consecration and Dedication of Two Certain Lots or Pieces of Ground as and for Cemeteries or Burial Grounds for the Interment of Persons Dying within the parish of Christ Church in the Island of New Providence One of the Bahama Islands within the Diocese of Jamaica," May 19, 1826, Records of the Anglican Diocese of Jamaica, Jamaica Archives, Spanish Town.

5. "Specifications for a Mortuary Chapel in Potter's Field or Western Cemetery," Ministry of Works Index, P. W. D. Minutes, Specs, Contracts, etc., 1863–1923, B18, Department of Archives, Nassau.

Chapter 4. St. Matthew's Northern Burial Ground

1. "An Act of Consecration and Dedication of Three Certain Lots or Pieces of Ground as of for Cemeteries or Burial Grounds for the Interment of Persons Dying Inhabitants of or within the Parish of Saint Matthew in the Island of New Providence, One of the Bahama Islands within the Diocese of Jamaica," May 20, 1826, Anglican Church Records— Bahamas, Jamaica Archives, Spanish Town.

2. "The Humble Petition of William Hepworth Officiating Minister and Andrew Seton and Dugald Blair Church Wardens and the Undersigned Magistrates and Inhabitants of the Parish of Saint Matthew in the Island of New Providence One of the said Bahama Islands on Behalf of Themselves and the Rest of the Inhabitants of the Said Parish," May 16, 1826, Anglican Church Records—Bahamas, Jamaica Archives, Spanish Town.

3. Christ Church was the earliest Anglican church in Nassau and the only church in Nassau with records that predate the Loyalist migration period. Christ Church Baptism Register, 1733–1840 and Christ Church Marriage Register, 1753–1805, Department of Archives, Nassau.

4. Christ Church Burial Registers, 1806–1814 and 1811–1828 (Whites) and 1814–1828 (Coloureds), Department of Archives, Nassau.

5. "Abutment (sea wall) first erected in 1883; Repair also in 1883," Index P. W. D. Minutes, Specs, Contracts, etc. 1863–1923, 5, Department of Archives, Nassau; "Specification of work required to be done in filling in & repairing the abutment (sea wall) in front of St. Matthews Burial Ground, July 1901," Ministry of Works Specification Book 1897–1902, 406–407, Department of Archives, Nassau.

6. St. Matthew's Church Minutes and Proceedings of the Vestry, 1802–1916, Department of Archives, Nassau.

7. Commissioners' Reports, Long Island District, 1922–1924, Department of Archives, Nassau.

8. Bahamas Statute Laws, Department of Archives, Nassau. See also Bahamas Historical Society (1968, 36).

Chapter 6. Interpretations of Artifacts and Ecofacts

1. Archaeology Lab Reference Collection, Colonial Williamsburg Foundation; Maryland Archaeological Conservation Laboratory (2002); Florida Museum of Natural History Digital Type Collections, Florida Museum of Natural History, http://www.flmnh.ufl.edu/histarch/gallery_types/.

2. Archaeology Lab Reference Collection, Colonial Williamsburg Foundation; Maryland Archaeological Conservation Laboratory (2002); Florida Museum of Natural History Digital Type Collections, Florida Museum of Natural History, http://www.flmnh.ufl.edu/histarch/gallery_types/.

3. Archaeology Lab Reference Collection, Colonial Williamsburg Foundation; Maryland Archaeological Conservation Laboratory (2002); Florida Museum of Natural History Digital Type Collections, Florida Museum of Natural History, http://www.flmnh.ufl.edu/histarch/gallery_types/; Nöel-Hume (1991, 134–136).

4. Archaeology Lab Reference Collection, Colonial Williamsburg Foundation; Maryland Archaeological Conservation Laboratory (2002).

5. Archaeology Lab Reference Collection, Colonial Williamsburg Foundation; Maryland Archaeological Conservation Laboratory (2002); Nöel-Hume (1991, 112–114).

6. Archaeology Lab Reference Collection, Colonial Williamsburg Foundation; Maryland Archaeological Conservation Laboratory (2002); Florida Museum of Natural History Digital Type Collections, Florida Museum of Natural History, http://www.flmnh.ufl.edu/histarch/gallery_types/; Nöel-Hume (1991, 133–134).

7. Archaeology Lab Reference Collection, Colonial Williamsburg Foundation; Maryland Archaeological Conservation Laboratory (2002); Florida Museum of Natural History Digital Type Collections, Florida Museum of Natural History, http://www.flmnh.ufl.edu/histarch/gallery_types/; Nöel-Hume (1991, 113–114).

8. Archaeology Lab Reference Collection, Colonial Williamsburg Foundation; Maryland Archaeological Conservation Laboratory (2002); Florida Museum of Natural History Digital Type Collections, Florida Museum of Natural History, http://www.flmnh.ufl.edu/histarch/gallery_types/; Nöel-Hume (1991, 122–123).

9. Archaeology Lab Reference Collection, Colonial Williamsburg Foundation; Florida Museum of Natural History Digital Type Collections, Florida Museum of Natural History, http://www.flmnh.ufl.edu/histarch/gallery_types/; Nöel-Hume (1991, 261–263).

10. Archaeology Lab Reference Collection, Colonial Williamsburg Foundation; Maryland Archaeological Conservation Laboratory (2002).

11. Archaeology Lab Reference Collection, Colonial Williamsburg Foundation; Maryland Archaeological Conservation Laboratory (2002); Florida Museum of Natural History Digital Type Collections, Florida Museum of Natural History, http://www.flmnh.ufl.edu/histarch/gallery_types/; Nöel-Hume (1991, 117).

12. Archaeology Lab Reference Collection, Colonial Williamsburg Foundation; Maryland Archaeological Conservation Laboratory (2002); Florida Museum of Natural History Digital Type Collections, Florida Museum of Natural History, http://www.flmnh.ufl.edu/histarch/gallery_types/; Nöel-Hume (1991, 114–116).

13. Archaeology Lab Reference Collection, Colonial Williamsburg Foundation; Florida Museum of Natural History Digital Type Collections, Florida Museum of Natural History, http://www.flmnh.ufl.edu/histarch/gallery_types/.

14. Archaeology Lab Reference Collection, Colonial Williamsburg Foundation; Maryland Archaeological Conservation Laboratory (2002); Florida Museum of Natural History Digital Type Collections, Florida Museum of Natural History, http://www.flmnh.ufl.edu/histarch/gallery_types/; Nöel-Hume (1991, 123–124).

15. Archaeology Lab Reference Collection, Colonial Williamsburg Foundation; Maryland Archaeological Conservation Laboratory (2002); Florida Museum of Natural History Digital Type Collections, Florida Museum of Natural History, http://www.flmnh.ufl.edu/histarch/gallery_types/; Nöel-Hume (1991, 124–126).

16. Archaeology Lab Reference Collection, Colonial Williamsburg Foundation; Florida Museum of Natural History Digital Type Collections, Florida Museum of Natural History, http://www.flmnh.ufl.edu/histarch/gallery_types/; Nöel-Hume (1991, 129–132).

17. Archaeology Lab Reference Collection, Colonial Williamsburg Foundation; Greer (1981, 75); Nöel-Hume (1991, 101).

18. Maryland Archaeological Conservation Laboratory (2002); Nöel-Hume (1991, 101).

19. Florida Museum of Natural History Digital Type Collections, Florida Museum of Natural History, http://www.flmnh.ufl.edu/histarch/gallery_types/.

Chapter 7. Conclusion

1. This transfer of title from the heirs of the lord proprietors to the British Crown is recorded in Book N, 229–259, Registrar General's Department, Nassau.

2. Gov. Thomas Shirley, Nassau, to the Earl of Hillsborough, Secretary of State for the Colonies, December 9, 1768, folio 7, Colonial Office CO23/8, folios 3–9, Department of Archives, Nassau.

3. Gov. Browne to the Earl of Dartmouth, folios 28–33, Colonial Office CO23/23, Department of Archives, Nassau.

4. The earliest surviving burial registers for Christ Church, which date to the early 1800s recorded white and nonwhite burials separately. Burial Registers, 1806–1814 (whites) and 1814–1828 (coloureds); Baptism Registers 1733–1840; Marriages Registers 1753–1805. All in Department of Archives, Nassau.

5. In the earliest surviving registers for St. Matthew's Church, which did not begin until 1802, recorded burials, marriages and baptisms for whites and nonwhites written in separate parts of the volumes. Department of Archives, Nassau.

6. St. Matthews Burial Ground Wall, 1906–1907, 29–30, Index for Ministry of Works, Index P. W. D. Minutes, Specs, Contracts, Etc. 1863–1923. Department of Archives, Nassau.

7. Overview of the truck system by Attorney General Matthews, August 10, 1907, Folios 335–336, Colonial Office CO23/262, Department of Archives, Nassau.

8. The 1807 Slave Trade Act authorized Royal Navy ships to rescue Africans from ships crossing the Atlantic illegally trading Africans as slaves. The first group of these "liberated" Africans were resettled in the Bahamas in 1811 as laborers apprenticed to masters for seven years or enlisted in the West India Regiment.

9. William Vesey Munnings, president of the Legislative Council, to the Earl of Liverpool, Secretary of State for the Colonies, August 22, 1811, Folios 30–31, CO23/58, Department of Archives, Nassau.

10. Governors' Despatches, 1823–1828, folios 1157–1168.

REFERENCES

Adderley, Rosanne Marion. 2006. *"New Negroes from Africa": Slave Trade Abolition and Free African Settlement in the Nineteenth-Century Caribbean.* Bloomington: Indiana University Press.

Armstrong, Douglas, and Mark Fleischman. 2003. House-Yard Burials of Enslaved Laborers in Eighteenth-Century Jamaica. *International Journal of Historical Archaeology* 7, no. 1: 33–65.

Bahamas, Department of Archives. 1986. *The Bahamas in the Late Nineteenth Century, 1870–1899.* Nassau: Department of Archives.

———. 1987. *The Bahamas during the Early Twentieth Century, 1900–1914.* Nassau: Department of Archives.

Bahamas Historical Society. 1968. *Nassau, Bahamas 1823–4: The Diary of a Physician from the United States Visiting the Island of New Providence.* Nassau: The Bahamas Historical Society.

Bahamas, Public Records Office. 1974. *The Sponging Industry.* Nassau, Bahamas: Public Records Office, Archives Section, Ministry of Education & Culture.

———. 1975. *A Selection of Historic Buildings of the Bahamas.* Nassau: Public Records Office, Archives Section

Bass, William. 2005. *Human Osteology: A Laboratory and Field Manual.* 5th ed. Columbia: Missouri Archaeological Society.

Battle-Baptiste, Whitney. 2011. *Black Feminist Archaeology.* New York: Routledge.

Beckles, Hillary. 2011. Servants and Slaves during the 17th-Century Sugar Revolution. In *The Caribbean: A History of the Region and Its People,* edited by Stephan Palmié and Francisco Scarano, 205–216. Chicago: University of Chicago Press.

Bender, Barbara, Sue Hamilton, and Chris Tilley. 2005. *Stone Worlds: Narrative and Reflexivity in Landscape Archaeology.* Walnut Creek, California.: Left Coast Press.

Birks, Steve. N.d. W H Grindley & Co (Ltd). *A–Z of Stoke-on-Trent Potters.* Accessed April 2012. http://www.thepotteries.org/allpotters/472.htm.

Blakey, Michael. 2001. Bioarchaeology of the African Diaspora in the Americas: Its Origins and Scope. *Annual Review of Anthropology* 30: 387–422.

Blakey, Michael, and Leslie Rankin-Hill, eds. 2009. *The Skeletal Biology of the New York*

African Burial Ground, Parts 1–2, volume 1 of *The New York African Burial Ground: Unearthing the African Presence in Colonial New York, Volume 1.* Washington, D.C.: Howard University Press, published in association with the United States General Services Administration.

Bloomingdale Brothers. (1886) 1988. *Bloomingdale's Illustrated 1886 Catalogue: Fashions, Dry Goods and Housewares.* Introduction by Nancy Villa Bryk. Published in association with Henry Ford Museum & Greenfield Village, Dearborn, Mich. New York: Dover Publications.

Blouet, Helen. 2010. Marking Life and Death on St. John, Virgin Islands, 1718–1950: An Historical Archaeology of Commemoration through Objects, Space, and Transformations. PhD diss., Syracuse University, Syracuse, New York.

———. 2014. Spatial and Material Transformations in Commemoration on St. John, U.S. Virgin Islands. In *Materialities of Ritual in Black America,* edited by Akinwumi Ogundiran and Paula Saunders, 280–295. Bloomington: Indiana University Press.

Bolton, H. Carrington. 1891. Decoration of Graves of Negroes in South Carolina. *Journal of American Folklore* 4, no. 14: 214.

Brathwaite, Edward Kamau. 1977. Caliban, Ariel, and Unprospro in the Conflict of Creolization: A Study of the Slave Revolt in Jamaica in 1831–32. In *Comparative Perspectives on Slavery in New World Plantation Societies,* edited by Vera Rubin and Arthur Tuden, 41–62. New York: New York Academy of Science.

Broome, R., K. Sabir, and S. Carrington. 2007. Plants of the Eastern Caribbean: Online Database (Beta). University of the West Indies, Cave Hill, Barbados. Accessed September 2012., http://ecflora.cavehill.uwi.edu/plantsearch.php?search_method=common_name&searchtxt=jumbie+lily&source=index&offset=0&rows=10.

Brown, Ras Michael. 2002. "Walk in the Feenda": West-Central Africans and the Forest in the South Carolina-Georgia Low Country. In *Central Africans and Cultural Transformations in the American Diaspora,* edited by L. M. Heywood, 289–317. Cambridge: Cambridge University Press.

Bruner, David E. 1996. Hidden Power: Burial Practices from an African-American Slave and Tenant Community. MA thesis, University of Houston, Houston, Texas.

Buckley, Roger Norman. 1979. *Slaves in Red Coats: The British West India Regiments, 1795–1815.* New Haven, Conn.: Yale University Press.

Cabrera, Lydia. 2004. *Afro-Cuban Tales.* Translated by Alberto Hernández-Chiroldes and Lauren Yoder. Lincoln: University of Nebraska Press. Originally published as *Cuentos negros de Cuba.*

Chenoweth, John M. 2009. Social Identity, Material Culture, and The Archaeology of Religion. *Journal of Social Archaeology* 9, no. 3: 319–340.

Chicora Foundation, Inc. 1996. Grave Matters: The Preservation of African-American Cemeteries. Accessed September 2012. http://www.sciway.net/hist/chicora/gravematters.html.

Chouin, Gérard. 2008. Archaeological Perspectives on Sacred Groves in Ghana. In *African Sacred Groves: Ecological Dynamics and Social Change,* edited by Michael Sheridan and Celia Nyamweru, 178–194. Oxford: James Currey.

Cohen, Hennig. 1958. Burial of the Drowned among the Gullah Negroes. *Southern Folklore Quarterly* 22:93–97.

Combes, John. 1974. Ethnography, Archaeology and Burial Practices among Coastal South Carolina Blacks. In *The Conference for Historic Site Archaeology Papers, 1972*, vol. 7, part 2, 52–61. Columbia: University of South Carolina.

Connor, Cynthia. 1989. Archaeological Analysis of African-American Mortuary Behavior. In *The Last Miles of the Way: African-American Homegoing Traditions, 1890–Present*, 51–55. Columbia: South Carolina State Museum.

Correll, Donovan, and Helen Correll. 1982. *Flora of the Bahama Archipelago: Including the Turks and Caicos Islands*. Vaduz: A. R. G. Gantner Verlag.

Craton, Michael, and Gail Saunders. 1992. *Islanders in the Stream: A History of the Bahamian People*. Vol. 1. Athens: University of Georgia Press.

Creel, Margaret Washington. 1988. *"A Peculiar People": Slave Religion and Community-Culture among the Gullahs*. New York: New York University Press.

David, Nicholas. 1992. The Archaeology of Ideology: Mortuary Practices in the Central Mandara Highlands, Northern Cameroon. In *An African Commitment: Papers in Honour of Peter Lewis Shinnie*, edited by Judy Sterner and Nicholas David, 181–210. Alberta: University of Calgary Press.

Davidson, James M. 2004. Mediating Race and Class through the Death Experience: Power Relations and Resistance Strategies of an African-American Community, Dallas, Texas (1869–1907). PhD diss., University of Texas at Austin.

DeCorse, Christopher. 2001. *An Archaeology of Elmina: Africans and Europeans on the Gold Coast, 1400–1900*. Washington, D.C.: Smithsonian Institution Press.

Deetz, James. 1996. *In Small Things Forgotten: An Archaeology of Early American Life*. Rev. ed. New York: Anchor Books.

Defoe, Daniel. 1999. *A General History of the Pyrates*. Edited by Manuel Schonhorn. Mineola, N.Y.: Dover Publications.

Delle, James A., and Kristen R. Fellows. 2014. Death and Burial at Marshall's Pen, a Jamaican Coffee Plantation, 1814–1839: Examining the End of Life at the End of Slavery. *Slavery & Abolition: A Journal of Slave and Post-Slave Studies* 35, no. 3: 474–492.

Department of Archives, Nassau. 1976. *St. Matthew's Cemetery and Eastern Burial Ground*. Nassau: Department of Archives.

———. 1982. *Settlements in New Providence*. Nassau: Department of Archives.

———. 1986. *The Bahamas during the Early Twentieth Century, 1900–1914*. Nassau: Department of Archives.

———. 1987. *The Bahamas in the Late Nineteenth Century, 1870–1899*. Nassau: Department of Archives.

Dockall, Helen Danzeiser, Joseph Powell, and Gentry Steele. 1996. *Home Hereafter: An Archaeological and Bioarchaeological Analysis of an Historic African-American Cemetery (41GV125), Reports of Investigations, No.5*. College Station: Center for Environmental Archaeology, Texas A&M University.

Douglass, Frederick. (1854) 1950. The Claims of the Negro Ethnologically Considered, Address Delivered at Western Reserve College, July 12. In *The Life and Writings of*

Frederick Douglass, vol. 2, *Pre-Civil War Decade 1850–1860*, edited by Philip Foner, 289–309. New York: International Publishers.

Du Bois, William Edward Burghardt. (1903) 1989. *The Souls of Black Folk*. New York: Penguin Books.

Eastwood, Jonathan. 2006. *The Rise of Nationalism in Venezuela*. Gainesville: University Press of Florida.

Eden, Edward. 2000. The Revolt on the Slave Ship *Creole*: Popular Resistance to Slavery in Post-Emancipation Nassau. *Bahamas Historical Society Journal* 22 (October): 13–20.

Emmet, Boris. 1969. *Montgomery Ward & Co.: Catalogue and Buyers' Guide No. 57, Spring and Summer 1895*. New York: Dover Publications.

Eneas, Cleveland W. (1976) 1988. *Bain Town*. Nassau: Cleveland and Muriel Eneas.

Epperson, Terrance. 2004. Critical Race Theory and the Archaeology of the African Diaspora. *Historical Archaeology* 38, no:1: 101–108.

Falola, Toyin. 2001. *Culture and Customs of Nigeria*. Westport, Conn.: Greenwood Press.

Farmer, Kevin, Frederick H. Smith, and Karl Watson. 2005. The Urban Context of Slavery: An Archaeological Perspective from two Afro-Barbadian Slave Cemeteries in Bridgetown, Barbados. In *Proceedings of the Twenty-First Congress of the International Association of Caribbean Archaeology*, 677–685. St. Augustine, Trinidad: University of the West Indies, School of Continuing Education.

Farnsworth, Paul. 1999. From the Past to the Present: An Exploration of the Formation of African-Bahamian Identity during Enslavement. In *African Sites: Archaeology in the Caribbean*, edited by Jay Haviser, 94–130. Princeton, N.J.: Marcus Weiner Publications.

Farquharson, Charles. 1957. *A Relic of Slavery: Farquharson's Journal for 1831–32*. Nassau: The Dean Peggs Research Fund.

Fenn, Elizabeth. 1989. Honoring the Ancestors: Kongo-American Graves in the American South. In *The Last Miles of the Way: African-American Homegoing Traditions, 1890–Present*, edited by Elaine Nichols, 44–50. Columbia: South Carolina State Museum.

Fennell, Christopher. 2003. Group Identity, Individual Creativity, and Symbolic Generation in a Bakongo Diaspora. *International Journal of Historical Archaeology* 7, no. 1: 1–31.

———. 2014. Dexterous Creation: Material Manifestations of Instrumental Symbolism in the Americas. In *Materialities of Ritual in Black America*, edited by Akinwumi Ogundiran and Paula Saunders, 216–235. Bloomington: Indiana University Press.

Ferguson, Leland. 1992. *Uncommon Ground: Archaeology and Early African America, 1650–1800*. Washington, D.C.: Smithsonian Institution.

Fesler, Garrett. 2004. From Houses to Homes: An Archaeological Case Study of Household Formation at the Utopia Slave Quarter, ca. 1675 to 1775. PhD diss., University of Virginia, Charlottesville.

Firmin, Anténor. (1885) 2002. *The Equality of the Human Races*. Urbana: University of Illinois Press.

Georgia Writers' Project, Savannah Unit, Work Projects Administration. 1972. *Drums and Shadows: Survival Studies among the coastal Georgia Negroes*. New York: Anchor Books.

GeoView, Inc. 2007. Final Report: Geophysical Investigation, The Northern Burial Ground of St. Matthew's Church Site, Nassau, Bahamas. Prepared for the National Museum of the Bahamas. St. Petersburg, Fla.: GeoView.

Gilchrist, Roberta, and Barney Sloane. 2005. *Requiem: The Medieval Monastic Cemetery in Britain*. London: Museum of London Archaeology Service.

Giles-Vernick, Tamara. 2002. *Cutting the Vines of the Past: Environmental Histories of the Central African Rain Forest*. Charlottesville: University Press of Virginia.

Gómez, Pablo. 2014. Transatlantic Meanings: African Rituals and Material Culture in the Early Modern Spanish Caribbean. In *Materialities of Ritual in the Black Atlantic*, edited by Akinwumi Ogundiran and Paula Saunders, 125–142. Bloomington: Indiana University Press.

Greene, Sandra. 2002. *Sacred Sites and the Colonial Encounter: A History of Meaning and Memory in Ghana*. Bloomington: Indiana University Press.

Greer, Georgeanna. 1981. *American Stoneware: The Art and Craft of Utilitarian Potters*. Exton: Schiffer Publishing Ltd.

Gundaker, Grey, and Judith McWillie. 2005. *No Space Hidden: The Spirit of African American Yard Work*. Knoxville: University of Tennessee Press.

Heath, Barbara, and Amber Bennett. 2000. "The little Spots Allow'd Them": The Archaeological Study of African-American Yards. *Historical Archaeology* 34, no. 2: 38–55.

Helg, Aline. 2004. *Liberty and Equality in Caribbean Colombia, 1770–1835*. Chapel Hill: University of North Carolina Press.

Herskovits, Melville Jean. 1941. *The Myth of the Negro Past*. New York: Harper and Brothers Publishers.

Higman, Barry W. 1984. *Slave Populations of the British Caribbean, 1807–1834*. Baltimore, Md.: Johns Hopkins University Press.

Holl, Augustin. 2001. 500 Years in the Cameroons: Making Sense of the Archaeological Record. In *West Africa during the Atlantic Slave Trade: Archaeological Perspectives*, edited by Christopher DeCorse, 152–78. London: Leicester University Press.

Howard, Rosalyn. 2002. *Black Seminoles in the Bahamas*. Gainesville: University Press of Florida.

Howard University and John Milner Associates. 1993. Research Design for Archaeological, Historical, and Bioanthropological Investigations of the African Burial Ground (Broadway Block) New York, New York. Prepared for the United States General Services Administration, Region 2.

Ingersoll, Ernest. 1892. Decoration of Negro Graves. *Journal of American Folklore* 5, no. 16: 68–69.

Israel, Fred, ed. 1968. *1897 Sears Roebuck Catalogue*. Chelsea House Publishers, New York.

Jamieson, Ross. 1995. Material Culture and Social Death: African-American Burial Practices. *Historical Archaeology* 29, no. 4: 39–58.

Johnson, David. 1948. *Uniform Buttons: American Armed Forces, 1784–1948*. 2 vols. Watkins Glen, N.Y.: Century House.

Johnson, Howard. 1996. *The Bahamas from Slavery to Servitude, 1783–1933*. Gainesville: University Press of Florida.

Johnson, Whittington B. 1996. The Amelioration Acts in the Bahamas, 1823–1833: A Middle Ground between Freedom and Antebellum Slave Codes. *Journal of the Bahamas Historical Society* 18 (October): 21–32.

———. 2001. Ownership of Slaves among Free Persons of Colour in the Bahamas. *Journal of the Bahamas Historical Society* 23: 32–38.

———. 2006. *Post-Emancipation Race Relations in the Bahamas*. Gainesville: University Press of Florida.

Jones, Olive. 1986. *Cylindrical English Wine and Beer Bottles, 1735–1850*. Ottawa: Ministry of the Environment. Accessed May 2012. http://www.sha.org/assets/documents/Cylindrical%20English%20Wine%20and%20Beer%20Bottles%20-%20English.pdf.

Jones, Olive, and Ann Smith. 1985. *Glass of the British Military, ca. 1755–1820*. Ottawa: Ministry of the Environment. Accessed June 2012. http://www.sha.org/assets/documents/Glass%20of%20the%20British%20Military%20-%20English.pdf.

Jones, Olive, and Catherine Sullivan, with contributions from George Miller, Ann Smith, Jane Harris, Kevin Lunn. 1989. *The Parks Canada Glass Glossary for the Description of Containers, Tableware, Flat Glass, and Closures*. Ottawa: Ministry of the Environment. Accessed June 2012. http://www.sha.org/assets/documents/The%20Parks%20Canada%20Glass%20Glossary.pdf.

Jordan, Terry. 1982. *Texas Graveyards: A Cultural Legacy*. Austin: University of Texas Press.

Keegan, William. 1997. *Bahamian Archaeology: Life in the Bahamas and Turks and Caicos before Columbus*. Nassau: Media Publishing.

Kelly, Kenneth. 2001. *Change and Continuity in Coastal Bénin*. In *West Africa during the Atlantic Slave Trade: Archaeological Perspectives*, edited by Christopher DeCorse, 81–100. London: Leicester University Press.

Khudabux, Mohammed. 1999. Effects of Life Conditions on the Health of a Negro Slave Community in Suriname. In *African Sites Archaeology in the Caribbean*, edited by Jay Haviser, 291–312. Princeton, N.J.: Markus Wiener Publishers.

LaCerte, Robert. 1993. The Evolution of Land and Labour in the Haitian Revolution, 1791–1820. In *Caribbean Freedom: Economy and Society from Emancipation to the Present*, edited by Hillary Beckles and Verene Sheperd, 42–47. Kingston: Ian Randle Publishers.

LaRoche, Cheryl, and Michael Blakey. 1997. Seizing Intellectual Power: The Dialogue at the New York African Burial Ground. *Historical Archaeology* 31, no. 3: 84–106.

Las Casas, Fray Bartolomé de. (1527–1562). 1965. *Historia de las Indias*. 3 vols. Edited by Agustín Millares Carlo. México: Fondo de Cultura Economica.

Lasso, Marixa. 2007. *Myths and Harmony: Race and Republicanism during the Age of Revolution, Colombia, 1795–1831*. Pittsburgh, Pa.: University of Pittsburgh Press.

Lefroy, John H. (1877). 1981. *Memorials of the Discovery and Early Settlement of the Bermudas or Somers Islands, 1515–1683*. Hamilton: Bermuda Historical Society and Bermuda National Trust.

Lenik, Stephan. 2005. Historical Archaeological Approaches to Tamarind Trees in the U.S. Virgin Islands. In *Proceedings of the Twenty-First Congress of the International Association of Caribbean Archaeology*, 31–40. St Augustine: University of the West Indies.

Levine, Robert. 1997. *Brazilian Legacies*. Armonk, N.Y.: M. E. Sharpe.

Little, Ruth. 1998. *Sticks and Stones: Three Centuries of North Carolina Grave Markers*. Chapel Hill: University of North Carolina Press.

Maceachern, Scott. 2001. State Formation and Enslavement in the Southern Lake Chad Basin. In *West Africa during the Atlantic Slave Trade: Archaeological Perspectives*, edited by Christopher DeCorse, 131–150. London: Leicester University Press.

MacGaffey, Wyatt. 1986. *Religion and Society in Central Africa: The BaKongo of Lower Zaire*. Chicago: University of Chicago Press.

Marotti, Frank, Jr. 2004. Freedom at Christmas: Andrew Gué, the Atlantic Community of Colour, and the "Underground Railroad" in the Bahamas, 1825–1844. *Journal of the Bahamas Historical Society* 26: 4–9.

Maryland Archaeological Conservation Laboratory. 2002. Diagnostic Artifacts in Maryland. Accessed September 2012. http://www.jefpat.org/diagnostic/Index.htm.

Marshall, Woodville. 1993. "We be wise to many more tings": Blacks' Hopes and Expectations of Emancipation. In *Caribbean Freedom: Economy and Society from Emancipation to the Present*, edited by Hillary Beckles and Verene Sheperd, 12–20. Kingston: Ian Randle Publishers.

Matternes, Hugh, and Staci Richey. 2014. "I Cry 'I Am' for All to Hear Me": The Informal Cemetery in Central Georgia. In *Materialities of Ritual in Black America*, edited by Akinwumi Ogundiran and Paula Saunders, 258–279. Bloomington: Indiana University Press.

Maxwell, Clarence V. H. 1999. Race and Servitude: The Birth of a Social and Political Order in Bermuda, 1619–1669. *Bermuda Journal of Archaeology and Maritime History* 11: 39–65.

McCarthy, John. 1996. Who Owns These Bones? Descendant Communities and Partnerships in the Excavation and Analysis of Historic Cemetery Sites in New York and Philadelphia. *Public Archaeology Review* 4, no. 2: 3–12.

———. 1997. Material Culture and the Performance of Sociocultural Identity: Community, Ethnicity, and Agency in the Burial Practices at the First African Baptist Church Cemeteries, Philadelphia, 1810–41. In *American Material Culture: The Shape of the Field*, edited by Anne Smart Martin and J. Ritchie Garrison, 359–380. Winterthur, Del.: Henry Francis du Pont Winterthur Museum.

———. 2006. African community identity at the cemetery. In *African Re-Genesis: Confronting Social Issues in the Diaspora*, edited by Jay Haviser and Kevin MacDonald, 176–183. Walnut Creek, Calif.: Left Coast Press.

McDermott, A. B., ed. 1960. *Nassau and the Bahama Islands* 12, no. 4: 27.

McNeil, Hope. 1998. *The Rituals Surrounding Birth and Death: A Jamaican Context*. MA thesis, Drew University, Madison, N.J.

McWeeney, Sean. 2002. Not Far from the Madding Crowd: Bahamian Reaction to the Revolutionary Upheaval in Haiti and the Intensification of Racial Control. *Journal of the Bahamas Historical Society* 24 (October): 17–27.

Medford, Edna Greene, ed. 2009. *Historical Perspectives of the African Burial Ground: New York Blacks and the Diaspora*, volume 3 of *The New York African Burial Ground*:

Unearthing the African Presence in Colonial New York. Washington, D.C.: Howard University Press, published in association with the United States General Services Administration.

Miller, George, Ann Smart Martin, and Nancy Dickinson. 1994. Changing Consumption Patterns: English Ceramics and the American Market from 1770 to 1840. In *Everyday Life in the Early Republic*, edited by Catherine Hutchins, 219–248. Winterthur, Del.: Henry Francis du Pont Winterthur Museum.

Mintz, Sidney W. (1974) 2006. *Caribbean Transformations*. New Brunswick, N.J.: Aldine Transaction.

Monroe, J. Cameron, and Akinwumi Ogundiran. 2012. Power and Landscape in Atlantic West Africa. In *Power and Landscape in Atlantic West Africa: Archaeological Perspectives*, edited by J. Cameron Monroe and Akinwumi Ogundiran, 1–45. New York: Cambridge University Press.

Morgan, Peter. 1999. The 32nd Regiment in the Bahamas, 1797–1799. *Journal of the Bahamas Historical Society* 21: 23–29.

Morris, Richard. 1983. *The Church in British Archaeology*. Research Report no. 47. London: Council for British Archaeology.

Nichols, Elaine, ed. 1989. *The Last Miles of the Way: African-American Homegoing Traditions, 1890–Present*. Columbia: South Carolina State Museum.

Nigh, Robin. 1997. Under Grave Conditions: African-American Signs of Life and Death in North Florida. *Markers XIV: Annual Journal of the Association for Gravestone Studies*: 158–189.

Noël-Hume, Ivor. 1991. *A Guide to Artifacts of Colonial America*. New York: Vintage Books.

Norman, Neil. 2014. Sacred Vortices of the African Atlantic World: Materiality of the Accumulated Aesthetic in the Hueda Kingdom, 1650–1727 CE. In *Materialities off Ritual in the Black Atlantic*, edited by Akinwumi Ogundiran and Paula Saunders, 47–67. Bloomington: Indiana University Press.

Ogundiran, Akinwumi, and Paula Saunders. 2014. On the Materiality of Black Atlantic Rituals. In *Materialities of Ritual in the Black Atlantic*, edited by Akinwumi Ogundiran and Paula Saunders, 1–27. Bloomington: Indiana University Press.

Oldmixon, John. (1741) 1969. *The British Empire in America*. New York: Augustus M. Kelley.

Orderson, J. W. (1842) 2002. *Creoleana: or Social and Domestic Scenes and Incidents in Barbados in Days of Yore and The Fair Barbadian and Faithful Black; or A Cure for the Gout*. Edited by John Gilmore. Oxford: Macmillan Publishers.

Orser, Charles E., Jr. 1998. The Archaeology of the African Diaspora. *Annual Review of Anthropology* 27: 63–82.

Outerbridge, Cyril Packwood. 1975. *Chained on the Rock: Slavery in Bermuda*. New York: Eliseo Torres & Sons.

Parsons, Elsie Clews. 1918. *Folk Tales of Andros Island, Bahamas*. New York: American Folklore Society.

Patten, M. Drake. 1997. Cheers of Protest? The Public, the *Post*, and the Parable of Learning. *Historical Archaeology* 31, no. 3: 132–139.

Perry, Warren, and Robert Paynter. 1999. Artifacts, Ethnicity, and the Archaeology of African Americans. In "I, Too, Am America": Archaeological Studies of African-American Life, 299–310. Theresa Singleton, ed. Charlottesville, University Press of Virginia.

Perry, Warren, Jean Howson, and Barbara Bianca, eds. 2009. The Archaeology of the New York African Burial Ground, Parts 1–3, volume 2 of The New York African Burial Ground: Unearthing the African Presence in Colonial New York. Washington, D.C.: Howard University Press, published in association with the United States General Services Administration.

Posnansky, Merrick. 1984. Toward an Archaeology of the Black Diaspora. Journal of Black Studies 15, no. 2: 195–205.

Powles, L. D. (1888) 1996. The Land of the Pink Pearl: Recollections of Life in the Bahamas. Nassau: Media Publishing.

Price, Richard. 1999. British Society, 1680–1880: Dynamism, Containment and Change. New York: Cambridge University Press.

Puckett, Newbell N. 1926. Folk Beliefs of the Southern Negroes. New York: Dover Books.

Rainville, Lynn. 2011. African-American Cemeteries in Albemarle and Amherst Counties. Accessed October 2012. http://www2.vcdh.virginia.edu/cem/AACemeteries_Landscape.shtml.

Rankin-Hill, Leslie. 1997. A Biohistory of 19th-Century Afro-Americans: The Burial Remains of a Philadelphia Cemetery. Westport, Conn.: Bergin & Garvey.

Reeves, Matthew. 2014. Mundane or Spiritual? The Interpretation of Glass Bottle Containers Found on Two Sites of the African Diaspora. In Materialities of Ritual in the Black Atlantic, edited by Akinwumi Ogundiran and Paula Saunders, 176–197. Bloomington: Indiana University Press.

Rodwell, Warwick. 1989. The Archaeology of Religious Places: Churches and Cemeteries in Britain. Philadelphia: University of Pennsylvania Press.

Ross, Eric. 2008. Palaver Trees Reconsidered in the Senegalese Landscape. In African Sacred Groves: Ecological Dynamics and Social Change, edited by Michael Sheridan and Celia Nyamweru, 133–148. Oxford: James Currey.

Rouse, Irving. 1992. The Tainos: Rise and Decline of the People Who Greeted Columbus. New Haven, Conn.: Yale University Press.

Rugg, Julie. 2000. Defining the Place of Burial: What Makes a Cemetery a Cemetery? Mortuary 5, no. 3: 259–275.

Sainsbury, W. Noel, ed. (1889) 1964. Calendar of State Papers: Colonial Series. Vol. 1, America and West Indies 1574–1660. Vaduz: Kraus Reprint.

Samford, Patricia M. 2000. Power Runs in Many Channels: Subfloor Pits and West African-Based Spiritual Traditions in Colonial Virginia. PhD diss., University of North Carolina at Chapel Hill.

Saunders, Gail. 1992. Bahamian Society after Emancipation. Kingston: Ian Randle Publishers.

Scarano, Francisco. 2011. Imperial Decline, Colonial Adaptation: The Spanish Islands during the Long 17th Century. In The Caribbean: A History of the Region and Its People, edited by Stephan Palmié and Francisco Scarano, 177–89. Chicago: University of Chicago Press.

Schoepf, Johann David. (1788) 1911. *Travels in the Confederation, 1783–1784*. Translated and edited by Alfred J. Morrison. Philadelphia: William J. Campbell.

Schuyler, Robert. 1980. *Archaeological Perspectives on Ethnicity in America: Afro-American and Asian-American Culture History*. Farmingdale, N.Y.: Baywood Publishing Company.

Sheridan, Michael. 2008. The Dynamics of African Sacred Groves: Ecological, Social and Symbolic Processes. In *African Sacred Groves: Ecological Dynamics and Social Change*, edited by Michael Sheridan and Celia Nyamweru, 9–41. Oxford: James Currey.

Singleton, Theresa. 2001. An Americanist Perspective on African Archaeology: Toward an Archaeology of the Black Atlantic. In *West Africa during the Atlantic Slave Trade: Archaeological Perspectives*, edited by Christopher DeCorse, 179–184. London: Leicester University Press.

Singleton, Theresa, and Mark Bograd. 1995. *The Archaeology of the African Diaspora in the Americas*. Ann Arbor, Mich.: Society for Historical Archaeology.

Skerry, Janine, and Suzanne Findlen Hood. 2010. *Salt-Glazed Stoneware in Early America*. Williamsburg, Va.: Colonial Williamsburg Foundation.

Smedley, Audrey. 1999. *Race in North America: Origin and Evolution of a Worldview*. Boulder, Colo. Westview Press.

Smith, Angèle. 2008. Landscapes of Clearance: Archaeological and Anthropological Perspectives. In *Landscapes of Clearance: Archaeological and Anthropological Perspectives*, edited by Angèle Smith and Amy Gazin-Schwartz, 13–24. Walnut Creek, California: Left Coast Press.

Smith, Jonathan. 2010. Hidden and Sacred: African American Cemeteries in East North Carolina. MA thesis, East Carolina University, Greenville.

Sobel, Mechal. 1988. *Trabelin' On: The Slave Journey to an Afro-Baptist Faith*. Princeton, N.J.: Princeton University Press.

Stahl, Ann Brower. 2001. Historical Process and the Impact of the Atlantic Trade on Banda, Ghana, c.1800–1920. In *West Africa during the Atlantic Slave Trade: Archaeological Perspectives*, edited by Christopher DeCorse, 38–58. London: Leicester University Press.

Sterner, Judy. 1992. Sacred Pots and "Symbolic Reservoirs" in the Mandara Highlands of Northern Cameroon. In *An African Commitment: Papers in Honour of Peter Lewis Shinnie*, edited by Judy Sterner and Nicholas David, 171–179. Alberta: University of Calgary Press.

Stevenson, Christopher. 2008. Burial Ground for Negroes, Richmond, Virginia: Validation and Assessment. Prepared for the Department of Historic Resources, Richmond, Virginia.

Themistocleous, Rosalyn. 1997. L. D. Powles, Stipendiary Magistrate. *Journal of the Bahamas Historical Society* 19 (October): 19–29.

Thompson, Robert Farris. 1984. *Flash of the Spirit: African and Afro-American Art and Philosophy*. New York: Vintage Books.

Thompson, Robert F., and Joseph Cornet. 1981. *The Four Moments of the Sun: Kongo Art in Two Worlds*. Washington, D.C.: Smithsonian Institution, National Gallery of Art.

Thompson, Sharyn. 2002. *Marriage, Birth and Death Notices from Newspapers of the Bahamas*. Tallahassee, Fla.: Off Island Press.

Thornton, John. 1998. *Africa and Africans in the Making of the Atlantic World, 1400–1800*. Cambridge: Cambridge University Press.

Tinker, Keith. 2011. *The Migration of Peoples from the Caribbean to the Bahamas*. Gainesville: University Press of Florida.

Turner, Grace. 2006. Bahamian Ship Graffiti. *International Journal of Nautical Archaeology* 35, no. 2: 253–273.

———. 2007. Bahamian Shipping in Black. Paper presented at the XXII Congress of the International Association for Caribbean Archaeology, July 23, Kingston, Jamaica.

Vivian, Brian. 1992. Sacred and Secular: Transitions in Akan Funerary Customs. In *An African Commitment: Papers in Honour of Peter Lewis Shinnie*, edited by Judy Sterner and Nicholas David, 157–167. Alberta: University of Calgary Press.

Vlach, John Michael. 1978. *The Afro-American Tradition in Decorative Arts*. Cleveland: Ohio: The Cleveland Museum of Art.

———. 1991. *By the Work of Their Hand: Studies in Afro-American Folklife*. Charlottesville: University Press of Virginia.

Wade, Peter. 1993. *Blackness and Race Mixture: The Dynamics of Racial Identity in Colombia*. Baltimore, Md.: Johns Hopkins University Press.

Walker, Phillip, Rhonda Bathurst, Rebecca Richman, Thor Gjerdrum, and Valerie Andrushko. 2009. The Causes of Porotic Hyperostosis and Cribra Orbitalia: A Reappraisal of the Iron-Deficiency-Anemia Hypothesis. *American Journal of Physical Anthropology* 139, no. 2: 109–125.

Wall, Diana diZerega. 1994. Family Dinners and Social Teas: Ceramics and Domestic Rituals. In *Everyday Life in the Early Republic*, edited by Catherine Hutchins, 249–284. Winterthur, Del.: Henry Francis du Pont Winterthur Museum.

Watters, David. 1994. Mortuary Patterns at the Harney Site Slave Cemetery, Montserrat, in Caribbean Perspective. *Historical Archaeology* 28, no. 3: 56–73.

Weiss, Brad. 2003. *Sacred Trees, Bitter Harvests: Globalizing Coffee in Northwest Tanzania*. Portsmouth, N.H.: Heinemann.

Whidden, Astrid. 1997. Key West Conchs, 1763–1912: Outlaws or Outcasts? *Journal of the Bahamas Historical Society* 19 (October): 30–43.

White, Tim. 2000. *Human Osteology*. 2nd ed. San Diego: Academic Press.

Wilkie, Laurie. 2000. *Creating Freedom: Material Culture and African-American Identity at Oakley Plantation, Louisiana, 1840–1950*. Baton Rouge: Louisiana State University Press.

Wilkie, Laurie, and Paul Farnsworth. 2005. *Sampling Many Pots: An Archaeology of Memory and Tradition at a Bahamian Plantation*. Gainesville: University Press of Florida.

Wilkinson, Henry Campbell. 1958. *The Adventurers of Bermuda: A History of the Island from Its Discovery until the Dissolution of the Somers Island Company in 1684*. Oxford: Oxford University Press.

Williams, Patrice M. (1979) 1991. *A Guide to African Villages in New Providence*. Nassau: Department of Archives.

———. 1999. *Chronological Highlights in the History of The Bahamas, 600–1900.* Nassau: Bahamas Historical Society.

Willsher, Betty. 2005. *Understanding Scottish Graveyards.* Edinburgh: Council for Scottish Archaeology and National Museums of Scotland.

Winer, Lise. 2009. *Dictionary of the English/Creole of Trinidad and Tobago: On Historical Principles.* Montreal: McGill-Queen's University Press.

Wood, David E. 1987. *A Guide to Selected Sources for the History of the Seminole Settlements at Red Bays, Andros, 1817–1980.* Nassau: Department of Archives.

Woodson, Carter G. 1937. Review of *Life in a Haitian Valley. Journal of Negro History* 22, no. 3: 366–369.

Wyckoff, Martin. 1984. *United States Military Buttons of the Land Services 1787–1902: A Guide and Classificatory System.* Bloomington, Ill.: McLean County Historical Society.

Wylly, William. 1789. *A Short Account of the Bahama Islands Their Climate, Productions, &c., to Which Are Added, Some Strictures upon Their Relative and Political Situation, the Defects of Their Present Government, &c. &c.* London.

Young, Jason. 2007. *Rituals of Resistance: African Atlantic Religion in Kongo and the Lowcountry South in the Era of Slavery.* Baton Rouge: Louisiana State University Press.

INDEX

Page numbers in *italics* refer to illustrations.

of, 17; Loyalists on, 17; map of, *12;* pirates and, 70; population on, 17, 19; roads on, 30; William Wylly's property on, 29

New Seville plantation, Jamaica, 46, 59, 64, 143

New York, NY: African Burial Ground in, 45, 47, 56, 73; and American Revolution, 95; black cemeteries in, 44, 45; and migration, 39

Nichols, Elaine, 55, 82

North Carolina, 107

Northern Burial Ground: 21st-century knowledge of, 74–75; as African-influenced cemetery, 72–73, 113, 141, 142, 146–47; Anglican Church and, 64, 143, 146; change in name of, 151n1 (intro); closing of, 143, 146; consecration of, 69, 70, 113; dating of, 98–99, 102, 103–4, 106, 107, 112–13, 141, 146; excavations of, 8, 9–10, 43–44, 45, 57, 78, 80–89, 123; and food offerings, 10, 80, 103, 115, 129, 140; free black settlements near, 113; GPR survey of, 8, 9, 74, 75, 76–78, *79,* 80, 87; and grave goods, 8, 99, 113, 140, 145–46; and grave plantings, 85, 88, 140; historical documentation on, 7, 69, 99; history of, 6–9; location of, 6, 7, 9, 56, 64, 70–71, 74–76, 81, 82, 115, 140, 141, 142; maintenance of, 73, 74, 99, 143; maps of, *71, 84;* photos of, 9, *75,* 78, *81, 84, 85, 86,* 87, *88, 89, 101;* scholarship on, 8; significance of, 3, 4, 6; threats to, 8, 57, 74, 78–79, 80, 83, 87, 88, 141; wall around, 143, 146

Northern Burial Ground, artifacts from: aluminum, 131; animal bones, 10, 80, 82, 83, 99, 126–30; Bakelite, 130; basalt, 137, 139; bottles, 82; brass, 130; brick, 10, 80, 89, 97; bricks, 131; buttons, 130, 131, 133–34; coins, 83, 130, 131; concrete, 131; copper/copper alloy, 130, 131, 133–34, *134;* coral, 137; crystalline stone, 131; cutlery, 83; dates of, 146; disc, 130; glass, 87, 99, 122–26, 131, 146; gold lace pin, 86, 92, 130, 132; headstones, 131, *135;* iron, 87, 89,

131; lead, 131, 134; limestone, 80, 83–85, 88, 89, 131, *135;* liquor bottle covers, 131; Lucayan, 82, 98, 136–39; marble, 131; nails, 97, 131; pewter, 130; photos and drawings of, *84, 88, 123, 124, 126, 128, 129, 132, 133, 134, 135, 138, 139;* plants, 137; plastic, 130, 131; plates, 130; porcelain, 131; pyrite, 131; rock, 137; shell, 82, 98, 130, 131, 133, 137; slate, 131; spikes, 87; stone, 82, 98, 131, 139; stud fastener, 130; treatment of, 9, 10, 83–85, 89, 126–27; utensil handles, 130, 134–35; utensils, 83; value of, 132; wood, 81–82, 131

Northern Burial Ground, ceramics from: American brown stoneware, 115; American stoneware, 110, 114, 120, 121; Astbury, 103–4, 114, 119, 122; bottles, 107, *108,* 117; bowls, 100, *105,* 115, 116, 117, 118, 119, 120, 136; Buckley-type stoneware, 105; Chinese porcelain, 104–5, 114, 117, 118, 120, 121, 122; chocolate pots, 119; coarse ceramic, 115, 120, 121; coffee pots, 119; creamware, 109, 114, 116, 117, 118, 119, 120, 121, 122; cups, 115, 117, 118; dates of, 83, 87, 98, 99–112, 113, 114–21, 141, 146; decoration on, 99–100, *101,* 103, 104, 105, 106, *108, 109,* 110, 111, 112, 116–21; dishes, 117, 119, 120, 121; drainage pipes, 120, 121; drinking vessels, 103; English brown stoneware, 114, 120, 122; flower pots, 119; Fulham-type stoneware, 102; gravel-tempered, 102–3, 114, 119, 122; griddles, 136; Guanajuato Majolica, 111, *112,* 114, 119, 122; hollow forms, 100, 103, 105, 116, 117, 118, 119, 120, 121; jars, 110, 120, 121; jugs, 117, 118, 119, 121; Lucayan, 99, 136–38; luster ware, 121, 122; manganese mottled ware, 101–2, 114, 120; milk pans, 100, 102–3, 107, 115; mugs, 115, 117, 118, 120; Nottingham stoneware, 103, 114, 119; opal glass/milk glass, 115, 121; pearlware, 109–10, 114, 116, 118, 119, 120, 121, 122; photos of, *100, 102, 103, 104, 105, 106, 107, 108, 109,*

GRACE TURNER, one of two Bahamian archaeologists who have currently earned a PhD, received a doctorate from the College of William & Mary in Williamsburg, Virginia, with a specialization in historical archaeology. While in Virginia, she worked for the Colonial Williamsburg Foundation in the Archaeology Lab. She was also an adjunct professor at Virginia Commonwealth University, Christopher Newport University, and the College of William & Mary. On returning to the Bahamas, she was contracted as chief archaeologist with the Antiquities, Monuments & Museum Corporation (AMMC). This quasi-government agency is responsible for archaeology, historic preservation, and government-funded museums in the Bahamas. As research consultant, Dr. Turner has updated historical information for brochures, exhibits, and historical reenactments at historic sites, particularly in Nassau.

Ripley P. Bullen Series

FLORIDA MUSEUM OF NATURAL HISTORY

Tacachale: Essays on the Indians of Florida and Southeastern Georgia during the Historic Period, edited by Jerald T. Milanich and Samuel Proctor (1978)

Aboriginal Subsistence Technology on the Southeastern Coastal Plain during the Late Prehistoric Period, by Lewis H. Larson (1980)

Cemochechobee: Archaeology of a Mississippian Ceremonial Center on the Chattahoochee River, by Frank T. Schnell, Vernon J. Knight Jr., and Gail S. Schnell (1981)

Fort Center: An Archaeological Site in the Lake Okeechobee Basin, by William H. Sears, with contributions by Elsie O'R. Sears and Karl T. Steinen (1982)

Perspectives on Gulf Coast Prehistory, edited by Dave D. Davis (1984)

Archaeology of Aboriginal Culture Change in the Interior Southeast: Depopulation during the Early Historic Period, by Marvin T. Smith (1987)

Apalachee: The Land between the Rivers, by John H. Hann (1988)

Key Marco's Buried Treasure: Archaeology and Adventure in the Nineteenth Century, by Marion Spjut Gilliland (1989)

First Encounters: Spanish Explorations in the Caribbean and the United States, 1492–1570, edited by Jerald T. Milanich and Susan Milbrath (1989)

Missions to the Calusa, edited and translated by John H. Hann, with an introduction by William H. Marquardt (1991)

Excavations on the Franciscan Frontier: Archaeology at the Fig Springs Mission, by Brent Richards Weisman (1992)

The People Who Discovered Columbus: The Prehistory of the Bahamas, by William F. Keegan (1992)

Hernando de Soto and the Indians of Florida, by Jerald T. Milanich and Charles Hudson (1992)

Foraging and Farming in the Eastern Woodlands, edited by C. Margaret Scarry (1993)

Puerto Real: The Archaeology of a Sixteenth-Century Spanish Town in Hispaniola, edited by Kathleen Deagan (1995)

Political Structure and Change in the Prehistoric Southeastern United States, edited by John F. Scarry (1996)

Bioarchaeology of Native American Adaptation in the Spanish Borderlands, edited by Brenda J. Baker and Lisa Kealhofer (1996)

A History of the Timucua Indians and Missions, by John H. Hann (1996)

Archaeology of the Mid-Holocene Southeast, edited by Kenneth E. Sassaman and David G. Anderson (1996)

The Indigenous People of the Caribbean, edited by Samuel M. Wilson (1997; first paperback edition, 1999)

Hernando de Soto among the Apalachee: The Archaeology of the First Winter Encampment, by Charles R. Ewen and John H. Hann (1998)

The Timucuan Chiefdoms of Spanish Florida, by John E. Worth: vol. 1, *Assimilation*; vol. 2, *Resistance and Destruction* (1998; first paperback edition, 2020)

Ancient Earthen Enclosures of the Eastern Woodlands, edited by Robert C. Mainfort Jr. and Lynne P. Sullivan (1998)

An Environmental History of Northeast Florida, by James J. Miller (1998)

Precolumbian Architecture in Eastern North America, by William N. Morgan (1999)

Archaeology of Colonial Pensacola, edited by Judith A. Bense (1999)

Grit-Tempered: Early Women Archaeologists in the Southeastern United States, edited by Nancy Marie White, Lynne P. Sullivan, and Rochelle A. Marrinan (1999; first paperback edition, 2001)

Coosa: The Rise and Fall of a Southeastern Mississippian Chiefdom, by Marvin T. Smith (2000)

Religion, Power, and Politics in Colonial St. Augustine, by Robert L. Kapitzke (2001)

Bioarchaeology of Spanish Florida: The Impact of Colonialism, edited by Clark Spencer Larsen (2001)

Archaeological Studies of Gender in the Southeastern United States, edited by Jane M. Eastman and Christopher B. Rodning (2001)

The Archaeology of Traditions: Agency and History Before and After Columbus, edited by Timothy R. Pauketat (2001)

Foraging, Farming, and Coastal Biocultural Adaptation in Late Prehistoric North Carolina, by Dale L. Hutchinson (2002)

Windover: Multidisciplinary Investigations of an Early Archaic Florida Cemetery, edited by Glen H. Doran (2002)

Archaeology of the Everglades, by John W. Griffin (2002; first paperback edition, 2017)

Pioneer in Space and Time: John Mann Goggin and the Development of Florida Archaeology, by Brent Richards Weisman (2002)

Indians of Central and South Florida, 1513–1763, by John H. Hann (2003)

Presidio Santa María de Galve: A Struggle for Survival in Colonial Spanish Pensacola, edited by Judith A. Bense (2003)

Bioarchaeology of the Florida Gulf Coast: Adaptation, Conflict, and Change, by Dale L. Hutchinson (2004; first paperback edition, 2020)

The Myth of Syphilis: The Natural History of Treponematosis in North America, edited by Mary Lucas Powell and Della Collins Cook (2005)

The Florida Journals of Frank Hamilton Cushing, edited by Phyllis E. Kolianos and Brent R. Weisman (2005)

The Lost Florida Manuscript of Frank Hamilton Cushing, edited by Phyllis E. Kolianos and Brent R. Weisman (2005)

The Native American World Beyond Apalachee: West Florida and the Chattahoochee Valley, by John H. Hann (2006)

Tatham Mound and the Bioarchaeology of European Contact: Disease and Depopulation in Central Gulf Coast Florida, by Dale L. Hutchinson (2007)

Taíno Indian Myth and Practice: The Arrival of the Stranger King, by William F. Keegan (2007; first paperback edition, 2022)

An Archaeology of Black Markets: Local Ceramics and Economies in Eighteenth-Century Jamaica, by Mark W. Hauser (2008; first paperback edition, 2013)

Mississippian Mortuary Practices: Beyond Hierarchy and the Representationist Perspective, edited by Lynne P. Sullivan and Robert C. Mainfort Jr. (2010; first paperback edition, 2012)

Bioarchaeology of Ethnogenesis in the Colonial Southeast, by Christopher M. Stojanowski (2010; first paperback edition, 2013)

French Colonial Archaeology in the Southeast and Caribbean, edited by Kenneth G. Kelly and Meredith D. Hardy (2011; first paperback edition, 2015)

Late Prehistoric Florida: Archaeology at the Edge of the Mississippian World, edited by Keith Ashley and Nancy Marie White (2012; first paperback edition, 2015)

Early and Middle Woodland Landscapes of the Southeast, edited by Alice P. Wright and Edward R. Henry (2013; first paperback edition, 2019)

Trends and Traditions in Southeastern Zooarchaeology, edited by Tanya M. Peres (2014)

New Histories of Pre-Columbian Florida, edited by Neill J. Wallis and Asa R. Randall (2014; first paperback edition, 2016)

Discovering Florida: First-Contact Narratives from Spanish Expeditions along the Lower Gulf Coast, edited and translated by John E. Worth (2014; first paperback edition, 2016)

Constructing Histories: Archaic Freshwater Shell Mounds and Social Landscapes of the St. Johns River, Florida, by Asa R. Randall (2015)

Archaeology of Early Colonial Interaction at El Chorro de Maíta, Cuba, by Roberto Valcárcel Rojas (2016)

Fort San Juan and the Limits of Empire: Colonialism and Household Practice at the Berry Site, edited by Robin A. Beck, Christopher B. Rodning, and David G. Moore (2016)

Rethinking Moundville and Its Hinterland, edited by Vincas P. Steponaitis and C. Margaret Scarry (2016; first paperback edition, 2019)

Gathering at Silver Glen: Community and History in Late Archaic Florida, by Zackary I. Gilmore (2016)

Paleoindian Societies of the Coastal Southeast, by James S. Dunbar (2016; first paperback edition, 2019)

Cuban Archaeology in the Caribbean, edited by Ivan Roksandic (2016)

Handbook of Ceramic Animal Symbols in the Ancient Lesser Antilles, by Lawrence Waldron (2016)

Archaeologies of Slavery and Freedom in the Caribbean: Exploring the Spaces in Between, edited by Lynsey A. Bates, John M. Chenoweth, and James A. Delle (2016; first paperback edition, 2018)

Setting the Table: Ceramics, Dining, and Cultural Exchange in Andalucía and La Florida, by Kathryn L. Ness (2017)

Simplicity, Equality, and Slavery: An Archaeology of Quakerism in the British Virgin Islands, 1740–1780, by John M. Chenoweth (2017)

Fit for War: Sustenance and Order in the Mid-Eighteenth-Century Catawba Nation, by Mary Elizabeth Fitts (2017)

Water from Stone: Archaeology and Conservation at Florida's Springs, by Jason O'Donoughue (2017)

Mississippian Beginnings, edited by Gregory D. Wilson (2017; first paperback edition, 2019)

Harney Flats: A Florida Paleoindian Site, by I. Randolph Daniel Jr. and Michael Wisenbaker (2017)

Honoring Ancestors in Sacred Space: The Archaeology of an Eighteenth-Century African-Bahamian Cemetery, by Grace Turner (2017; first paperback edition, 2023)

Investigating the Ordinary: Everyday Matters in Southeast Archaeology, edited by Sarah E. Price and Philip J. Carr (2018)

New Histories of Village Life at Crystal River, by Thomas J. Pluckhahn and Victor D. Thompson (2018)

Early Human Life on the Southeastern Coastal Plain, edited by Albert C. Goodyear and Christopher R. Moore (2018; first paperback edition, 2021)

The Archaeology of Villages in Eastern North America, edited by Jennifer Birch and Victor D. Thompson (2018)

The Cumberland River Archaic of Middle Tennessee, edited by Tanya M. Peres and Aaron Deter-Wolf (2019)

Pre-Columbian Art of the Caribbean, by Lawrence Waldron (2019)

Iconography and Wetsite Archaeology of Florida's Watery Realms, edited by Ryan Wheeler and Joanna Ostapkowicz (2019)

New Directions in the Search for the First Floridians, edited by David K. Thulman and Ervan G. Garrison (2019)

Archaeology of Domestic Landscapes of the Enslaved in the Caribbean, edited by James A. Delle and Elizabeth C. Clay (2019; first paperback edition, 2022)

Cahokia in Context: Hegemony and Diaspora, edited by Charles H. McNutt and Ryan M. Parish (2020)

Bears: Archaeological and Ethnohistorical Perspectives in Native Eastern North America, edited by Heather A. Lapham and Gregory A. Waselkov (2020)

Contact, Colonialism, and Native Communities in the Southeastern United States, edited by Edmond A. Boudreaux III, Maureen Meyers, and Jay K. Johnson (2020)

An Archaeology and History of a Caribbean Sugar Plantation on Antigua, edited by Georgia L. Fox (2020)

Modeling Entradas: Sixteenth-Century Assemblages in North America, edited by Clay Mathers (2020)

Archaeology in Dominica: Everyday Ecologies and Economies at Morne Patate, edited by Mark W. Hauser and Diane Wallman (2020)

The Making of Mississippian Tradition, by Christina M. Friberg (2020)

The Historical Turn in Southeastern Archaeology, edited by Robbie Ethridge and Eric E. Bowne (2020)

Falls of the Ohio Archaeology: Archaeology of Native American Settlement, edited by David Pollack, Anne Tobbe Bader, and Justin N. Carlson (2021)

A History of Platform Mound Ceremonialism: Finding Meaning in Elevated Ground, by Megan C. Kassabaum (2021)

New Methods and Theories for Analyzing Mississippian Imagery, edited by Bretton T. Giles and Shawn P. Lambert (2021)

Methods, Mounds, and Missions: New Contributions to Florida Archaeology, edited by
   Ann S. Cordell and Jeffrey M. Mitchem (2021)
Unearthing the Missions of Spanish Florida, edited by Tanya M. Peres and Rochelle A.
   Marrinan (2021)
Presidios of Spanish West Florida, by Judith A. Bense (2022)
En Bas Saline: A Taíno Town before and after Columbus, by Kathleen Deagan (2023)
Mississippian Women, edited by Rachel V. Briggs, Michaelyn Harle, and Lynne P.
   Sullivan (2024)

www.ingramcontent.com/pod-product-compliance
Lightning Source LLC
Chambersburg PA
CBHW070333270326
41926CB00017B/3859

* 9 7 8 1 6 8 3 4 0 4 0 4 0 *